MESSAGE OF BIBLICAL SPIRITUALITY
Editorial Director: Carolyn Osiek, RSCJ

Volume 2

Temple, Monarchy and Word of God

John Endres, S.J.

Michael Glazier
Wilmington, Delaware

ABOUT THE AUTHOR

John Endres, S.J. is on the faculties of the Jesuit School of Theology and the Graduate Theological Union in Berkeley, California. He has done biblical studies at the Hebrew University in Jerusalem, Weston School of Theology in Cambridge, Massachusetts, and received a doctorate in Old Testament at Vanderbilt University in Nashville, Tennessee (1982). Among his publications is *Biblical Interpretation in the Book of Jubilees*.

First published in 1988 by Michael Glazier, Inc., 1935 West Fourth Street, Wilmington, Delaware 19805.

Copyright ©1988 by Michael Glazier, Inc. All rights reserved.

Library of Congress Catalog Card Number: 87-83356

International Standard Book Number:

    Message of Biblical Spirituality series:

                0-89453-550-1, cloth; 0-89453-566-8, paper.

    TEMPLE MONARCHY/GOD:

                0-89453-552-8, cloth; 0-89453-568-4, paper.

Typography by Laura Kay Burke. Cover design by Florence Bern.

Printed in the United States of America.

TABLE OF CONTENTS

FOREWORD

Some of the questions we ask others return later to haunt us. The process of imagining and writing this book has proven to be such an experience for me. As I complete this volume, I am reminded of a question I have posed several times for doctoral students in Christian spirituality here in the Graduate Theological Union.

> The 1983 Code of Canon Law of the Roman Catholic Church includes the following canon: "The Christian faithful have the right . . . to follow their own form of spiritual life consonant with the teaching of the Church" [#214].[1] Could this particular canon be rooted in the witness of the Scriptures? Has your study of the biblical foundations of spirituality provided a basis for such an affirmation? Please include specific references to biblical texts.

If my exploration of the Books of Samuel, Kings, and Chronicles has taught me anything significant, it is simply this: these books witness to a variety of healthy ways to live out one's faith vision. For me, these books affirm the healthy

---

[1]*Code of Canon Law: Latin-English Edition* (Washington, DC: Canon Law Society of America, 1983), p. 73.

spiritual diversity which many people experience and foster today.

The way that this viewpoint emerged in my working still surprises me. As the series editor and I corresponded about an appropriate title for this volume, I felt a need to focus not only on temple and monarchy in ancient Israel, but also on the prophetic word of God which plays such an important role in these books. Gradually we came to agree on the present title, and then I was left with the task of discovering how each of these terms played an important role in these books. In this case, the title of the work came first and it really helped me to shape my own vision of Israel's spiritualities during these years.

I began to realize that I was dealing with very different ways of living in ancient Israel. Temple, monarchy, and word of God each represent distinct settings and avenues for those in search of meaning, identity, and relationship with God. I will suggest that these models or metaphors resemble what we in later centuries call spiritualities. Each of them grasps an angle of the truth, though none exhausts it. So I came to find one answer to the very question I had asked of others: here are books which speak eloquently of the different ways to live out faith-filled lives, different types of spirituality. That realization, of course, pleases me much more than finding biblical evidence for canon law!

Similarly, a variety of alternative spiritualities presents itself to us. In the process of developing our own spiritual vision, we recognize that our degree of freedom depends on many factors, including the familial and cultural situation into which we are born, and where we were nourished and educated. Our own possibilities are both restricted and expanded by those institutions which form the horizons of our lives. I hope that this focus on Israel's institutions—temple, monarchy, word of God—will help us to enter our own spiritual world as well as Israel's.

As I look back on my writing journey, I want to recognize helpers on the way. I am grateful to Carolyn Osiek for the invitation to prepare this volume in the series which she is editing, as well as for ongoing encouragement and patience with my time schedule. A bit later I was able to offer a seminar here with a title which bears striking resemblance to that of this volume! My students in that class challenged and helped me to develop a vision of the spirituality of these books. One of them, Keith Langstaff, read the first draft last summer and offered helpful comments and encouragement. Since I was not writing for a group of biblical professionals, I engaged others in conversation about my project. Elizabeth Liebert kept questioning me about my view of spirituality—even after reading the first draft! My father spent part of our summer visit together trying to make sense of what I'd written. I want to acknowledge the expert editorial assistance I received from Jean Blomquist. Finally, I am grateful for the Lilly Foundation grant for faculty development at the Jesuit School of Theology at Berkeley, and to my dean, Hal Sanks, for directing some of those funds to the completion of this project.

Each of these persons will, I hope, recognize their contributions to this book. Even more important, I hope my reading of these Scriptures helps them to find their own spirituality and appreciate it more deeply. This writing has done that for me. My hope is that all those who read these Scriptures along with me will discover the beauty of their own "place."

SPIRITUALITY AND BIBLICAL STORY

Spirituality means many different things to different people. For some people, this term evokes memories of devotions and novenas, of conscious attempts to set aside time for prayer and renewal. For others, it recalls special traditions or various "schools" of spirituality, many of them co-existing within the scope of the Catholic Church. For this book, I understand spirituality as the way in which one actually lives one's life, based on one's world-view and self understanding—and both of them in relation to God. How we think about ourselves and God, what we value, and the actions we undertake all combine to form our spirituality.

In Christian history there are some groups who share a special vision of life, a common spirituality. Some people call them 'schools' of spirituality. Some "schools" are well known, such as Benedictine spirituality, Franciscan spirituality, Ignatian spirituality, or the spirituality of Francis de Sales. For each of these "schools" a founder's life defines the different ideas of spirituality. For example, Benedict handed down a very different set of spiritual teachings than did Francis of Assisi. People in each of these traditions live according to a very different set of spiritual teachings.

Each of these 'schools' also fits best for those in a particular life-style. Many groups of monks and nuns stress the regular daily cycle of prayer and work, following the example and teaching of Benedict. Traditionally, mendicants were those who relied on alms for their sustenance. Generally they opt for a life that is less financially secure and which allows them to move easily to many different places. They find exceptional nourishment and example in the lives of Clare and Francis of Assisi, as well as from Dominic. Apostolic groups are those which offer themselves for works which meet the specific pastoral needs of a particular time or place. These groups often draw their encouragement from the life and example of people like Elizabeth Ann Seton or Ignatius of Loyola. Perhaps the most attractive, though least widely known of all the traditions I have mentioned, is that of Francis de Sales. Written mainly for lay people, his teaching stresses the importance and holiness of many different and complementary life-styles—not just those of religious and the ordained ministers of the church community.

Spiritualities such as these derive much of their strength and attraction from the life and story of a person who models a special way of living the life of faith. Their teachings and tradition are rooted in everyday life and choices. Spirituality begins with human life and experience; these form primary resources for the life of faith, drawn by the Spirit.

Spirituality and Story

Stories are the regular vehicles for handing on traditions about a person's life and vision. When we investigate our family histories, the family tree—with its copious genealogies and chronologies—stands side by side with stories about our forebears. Both types of information fulfill personal needs: we wish to know who our ancestors were, when they lived, and also what kind of people they were. From stories and narratives we learn about them, their personalities and achievements, strengths and weaknesses. Many details cannot be verified with historical precision; perhaps the precise dates and settings are not available, or we have received erroneous information. But the stories remain, and we hand them on because we are interested in people, how they live, and what they value.

When it comes to family, strict historical investigation usually stands in a position of secondary importance. Times and places of events do concern us, but ethnic background and gender differences also influence us. For example, my grandfather worked for several companies during his life, but the names of those firms and the dates he worked for them do not interest me as much as the type of jobs he held and how he performed them. My grandmother became a Roman Catholic after the birth of all her children, but the fact of her "conversion" interests me far less than her motives for taking that step. The absence of a local Protestant church was a major factor. Learning the 'hows' and the 'whys' of their lives offers deeper insight into their spirituality than do the bare facts of their lives.

When a family gathers, we often tell stories about our ancestors. We who hear and retell the stories can laugh at their foibles—and ours. Within the family, the 'hows' of their lives help us to understand and evaluate our own. We can try to avoid their mistakes, patterning our lives after their achievements—or the opposite. The family 'history' provides information, while the history-like story opens up life to us.

When the stories handed on involve faith in God and life directed by the Spirit of God, they become bearers of a spirituality. When we hand on such stories, we ourselves are preserving spiritual traditions. The *Lives of the Saints* have nurtured generations of Catholics, offering examples of a way of living—a spirituality for life. Technical history of the saints, written by researchers, seems far less important to most of us than the religious values their lives offer us. For example, why do so many people miss "Saint Christopher" in the current liturgical calendar? Is it not because we still cherish the religious value his story symbolizes for us: as a way of serving God, he calls us to courageous assistance to those imperilled in travel. Generations of Catholic children learned the Greek etymology of this name. Christopher means 'Christ-bearer', and his bearing of the Christ-child should inspire us to assist others with similar generosity. Those who continue to wear St. Christopher medals, then, make no historical judgment; in his heroic story, they find courage and hope for their own lives. Whether he lived or not seems less important than the wonderful example of Christian life which this story offers us.

Those who retell lives of famous saints often present a variety of perspectives on the saints whom they portray. St. Gregory the Great tells a story about Benedict and Scholastica. When I first heard it, I recall identifying first with one, then with the other character of the story. Here is the story.

> Scholastica, the sister of Saint Benedict, had been consecrated to God from her earliest years. She was accustomed to visiting

her brother once a year. He would come down to meet her at a place on the monastery property, not far outside the gate.

One day she came as usual and her saintly brother went with some of his disciples; they spent the whole day praising God and talking of sacred things. As night fell they had supper together.

Their spiritual conversation went on and the hour grew late. The holy nun said to her brother: "Please do not leave me tonight; let us go on until morning talking about the delights of the spiritual life." "Sister," he replied, "what are you saying? I simply cannot stay outside my cell."

When she heard her brother refuse her request, the holy woman joined her hands on the table, laid her head on them and began to pray. As she raised her head from the table, there were such brilliant flashes of lightning, such great peals of thunder and such a heavy downpour of rain that neither Benedict nor his brethren could stir across the threshold of the place where they had been seated. Sadly he began to complain: "May God forgive you, sister. What have you done?" "Well," she answered, "I asked you and you would not listen; so I asked my God and he did listen. So now go off, if you can, leave me and return to your monastery."

Reluctant as he was to stay of his own will, he remained against his will. So it came about that they stayed awake the whole night, engrossed in their conversation about the spiritual life.[2]

Benedict's dilemma parallels situations most of us have experienced in our lives, when legitimate requests and expectations seem to conflict with our duties. Predicaments like Benedict and Scholastica's intrigue us because of the

[2]"From the Book of the Dialogues by Saint Gregory the Great, pope," *The Liturgy of the Hours III* (New York: Catholic Book Publishing Company, 1975), pp. 1372-73.

different values they embody. In their story, both sets of values are good in themselves—observing the monastic rule versus spending quality time conversing with loved ones. We would like to avoid choosing between them. In this story, choosing the better of two goods really is an issue of spiritual discernment, and we can observe the process in action.

The storyteller presents the different values in a concrete situation through dialogue and description. We learn that they met "outside the gate" of the monastery, as is proper. Benedict exclaims to his sister: "I simply cannot stay outside my cell." The monastic viewpoint appears obliquely in this story, and since it constitutes the context of his choice we say that Benedict acts according to his monastic spirituality. Stories such as this could encourage a person struggling to live out the responsibilities of commitments, job, or ministry.

Scholastica's life-style was also prescribed by the monastic rule. The basic 'fact' of her life as a nun is stated simply: she was "consecrated to God from her earliest years." But the story also hints at her primary concern: "Let us go on until morning talking about the delights of the spiritual life." Here the narrator surprises us. Scholastica's way of proceeding, her particular spirituality, derives not from our understanding of monastic life but from her actions on this occasion. Her delights in life become the object of her desire on this occasion and they lead her to prayer. For many of us, Scholastica's example may prove nourishing as we try to follow deep, God-given desires which seem to conflict with other expressions of faithful life-styles. The criterion by which she acts witnesses to a spirituality which differs slightly from her brother's, and perhaps from many sisters in her own religious community.

Perhaps we could further distinguish the perspectives of these two characters. Scholastica speaks and acts primarily in relational terms, as she focuses on her relationships with Benedict and with God: she desires a longer conversation with her brother, and she asks God for what delights her. Benedict, on the other hand, lives according to the dictates of monastic rule and invokes God only to discourage his sister's enthusiasm and hopes. While the storyteller manifests a bias for Scholastica's action and spirituality, he presents both of them sympathetically. Benedict's spirituality is not maligned, though it does not provide the best criterion for this particular choice.

The story includes at least two spiritualities, those of the two main characters. We know these spiritualities by the dialogue and actions of the main characters. At a deeper level we realize that their choices and decisions are guided by the ways in which they see themselves. Benedict views himself primarily as a monk, while Scholastica sees herself first in relationship with him and then with God.

This charming story from the early Middle Ages might help us to reflect on our own spiritualities. Our perspectives on ourselves, our particular ways of life, even our social and economic situations all combine to form the warp and woof of our spiritual lives. The characters in this story help us to ask where we stand, how we might be ourselves, what forms our basic spiritualities.

But the story is incomplete. When I presented it above, I omitted its conclusion. Let us consider it now.

It is not surprising that she was more effective than he; since, as John says, "God is love," it was absolutely right that she could do more, as she loved more.

Three days later, Benedict was in his cell. Looking up to the sky, he saw his sister's soul leave her body in the form of a dove, and fly up to the secret places of heaven. Rejoicing in her great glory, he thanked almighty God with hymns and words of praise. He then sent his brethren to bring her body to the monastery and lay it in the tomb he had prepared for himself.

Their minds had always been united in God; their bodies were to share a common grave.[3]

Now the storyteller draws some conclusions about this incident and gently turns the story into a little homily about the ways in which we might live our own lives. Gregory comments on the outcome of the story: God heard and answered Scholastica's plea because she acted out of love. Her joy in conversation, her delights and desires become an occasion for the storyteller to become a homilist. Gregory explains how the love of God, so cherished in the writings of John the evangelist, emerges in the experience of this heroine of the Christian life. At the same time, he suggests to his hearers how they might incarnate God's love in their lives. Gregory acts like a preacher, presenting through the story a way of living, a genuine spirituality for life. Like his first audience, we too might learn from Gregory, from Benedict, and from Scholastica how to enflesh God's love in our lives. The power of a story like this can span the centuries which separate us from them. So, a third spirituality has emerged in this "saintly tale".

[3]*Ibid.*

Let us reflect on the process we have undergone as I recounted this story and explained its significance. The story itself contained a concrete situation in which major characters acted in accord with their own spiritualities. Within the story the actors presented different ways of life, each of which was authentic and based on an experience of God. That which distinguished their actions was as important as the faith they shared: they acted in accord with the primary way that they viewed themselves in relation to each other and to God. The way of living according to which each proceeded drew both on their life situations and on the personal meaning each had found for his or her life. This is how I have described spirituality.

The storyteller also adds his own interpretation of the narrative: "she could do more, as she loved more." Gregory's text presents both story and interpretation in this vignette about Scholastica and Benedict. Moreover, we discovered at least three spiritualities in his retelling of the story. The story contains spiritualities for both Benedict and Scholastica, and a third appears in the narrator's comments. The former two spiritualities relate directly to the life-settings and personalities of the characters; the latter is identified through reflection on his comments. We can find direction and inspiration not only in Gregory's sermon-like remarks, but also in the story itself. This story shows us how to read carefully, to discover both story and interpretation in a text. Even more importantly, it shows how a story can manifest different spiritualities, and when someone retells it with a moral, he or she can add a further spiritual vision for us.

In this book I will distinguish between the spirituality of the story and the spirituality of the interpreter. We can do this by separating—as far as it is possible—the narratives in the books of Samuel, Kings, and Chronicles from the commentaries discovered within them. I will call those ways of living discovered within biblical story a *narrative spirituality.* Or perhaps it would be better to speak of *narrative spiritualities,* since we can usually find different ways of faithful living represented in the same story. When I reflect on the interpretive contributions to a story, I will speak of *homiletic spirituality.*

Biblical Story and Spirituality

Let us linger with these two kinds of spirituality to see how they might emerge from biblical books. Gregory's discourse, which we have examined, can suggest ways of reading biblical texts more fruitfully. In my reading of Israel's historical books, I discover several different spiritualities. Within the narratives in Samuel, Kings, and Chronicles, many characters or actors display ways of living and relating to God. In their stories we may find spiritualities. But when I read these books I also find numerous comments on the stories they contain; like Gregory's moralizing, these remarks interpret the history-like story which they accompany. These six books of the Bible contain both story and interpretation, and each level of the text offers a spiritual vision, accompanied by examples for reflection.

Returning to the family setting, we recognize similar motives at work in the storytelling which occurs at gatherings and becomes part of family history. People tell stories because they delight the hearers and teach them about their roots, where they have come from, what kind of people their ancestors were. By telling stories, we learn a great deal. Yet storytellers often retell particular stories because they so nicely suit a contemporary situation or dilemma. Sometimes narrators explain why they choose this story; they point to the meaning of the narrative for its hearers. Although we never use such terms, families who retell their history may engage in the communication of spirituality when they retell their old stories. If their stories communicate a way of living in which faith in God plays a part, we speak of narrative spirituality in these stories. On the other hand, if their interpretation contains mention of God's ways or invitations or commands, we can speak of a homiletic spirituality in the family history.

For the purposes of this book, the family which interests us is the faith community of Israel, and its descendants throughout the ages, both Jewish and Christian. The "family history" of this group appears mainly in the Old Testament, especially in those books which narrate Israel's history. We now turn to those biblical books which are the focus of this volume: 1-2 Samuel, 1-2 Kings, 1-2 Chronicles. These six books of Israel's family history purport to present Israel's history for later generations. As we find these books now, they seem to come from two distinct histories, the History of the Deuteronomists [Deuteronomy, Joshua, Judges, 1-2 Samuel, 1-2 Kings] and the Chronicler's History [1-2 Chronicles, Ezra, Nehemiah]. Although the Book of Chronicles repeats much of the history found in 1-2 Samuel and 1-2 Kings, there are enough differences in content, outlook and spirituality to suggest that they are works from distinct times, places, and writers. Though we rely on other sources for much of our historical information, these books provide the basic outline of the history of the monarchic era. A chronological outline of this history appears in Appendix I.

CONTENTS OF 1-2 SAMUEL AND 1-2 KINGS

For the faith community which finds spiritual nourishment in these Scriptures, an historical chart (like that in Appendix 1) functions somewhat like a family tree, complete with genealogical and chronological tables. Such lists entice the reader to search out the story behind the facts. The books of Samuel, Kings, and Chronicles contain a history-like story, a narrative of the life and times of Israel during the era of the monarchy. This period stretches from Saul and David (around 1000 BCE) to the last king of Judah, Jehoiachin (587 BCE). These books recount events and persons in both of the kingdoms which resulted from the split after the death of Solomon—Judah in the south and Israel in the north. This is the era of the first temple and of the major prophets who proclaim the word of God in Israel.

The books of Samuel begin with the emergence of the prophet Samuel. His life forms the transition between rule under the judges [described in the Book of Judges] and by the kings [1 Sam 1-7]. The narratives about King Saul, his installation, leadership, and decline due to his loss of God's favor follow [1 Sam 8-15]. David's election by the aged Samuel, his rise to power in spite of Saul's opposition, and his troubled reign in Israel contain the largest amount of material in these two books [1 Sam 16-31; 2 Sam 1-24]. Devoted almost entirely to David, these books suggest his tremendous influence on Israel's imagination and spirituality.

The books of Kings follow, presenting a chronicle of the kingdoms of Judah in the south and—after Solomon's death and Jeroboam's secession—Israel in the north. After David, Solomon receives the most attention [1 Kgs 3-11]. Several kings receive slightly more attention than the rest: Ahab, Hezekiah, Manasseh, and Josiah. The other main characters of this unfolding story are prophets, those who proclaim God's word. Most prominent among them are Nathan, Elijah, and Elisha. Later rulers in Israel and Judah generally receive only brief notice; their reigns were often judged by their concern for the temple and Torah. The books of Kings conclude with the description of Babylon's conquest of Judah and a sketchy view of life after the destruction of Jerusalem and during the exilic era.

CONTENTS OF 1-2 CHRONICLES

The books of Chronicles contain a history which spans the time from the creation of the world through the fall of Jerusalem in 587 BCE. They do not give equal treatment to every period of Israel's history. For example, 1 Chronicles 1-9 treats the period from the creation of the world to the time of King Saul by presenting extensive genealogies; no stories are included. First Chronicles 10-29 describes the rise of David and his rule, paying special attention to his concern for the construction of the future temple and provision of its personnel [1 Chr 22-29].

Second Chronicles 1-9, describes Solomon's reign, seen as a kind of golden age for later Israel to remember and to anticipate again. The remainder of 2 Chronicles covers history following Solomon's reign. It focuses on the southern kingdom of Judah, and the exemplary lives and reigns of Kings Jehoshaphat, Hezekiah, and Josiah, contrasting them with the evil reign of Manasseh. The Chronicler maintains hope for a reunion of all Israel, that is both the southern and northern kingdoms. Like 2 Kings, this narrative continues until the account of the Exile to Babylon. Unlike 2 Kings, Chronicles concludes with the decree of Cyrus [2 Chr 36:22-23], which charges the Exiles to return to Jerusalem and Judah. In summary, the Chronicler's history covers the Pentateuch by way of genealogies and the History of the Deuteronomists by rewriting the story with special emphasis on David's royal line.

BIBLICAL STORY AND INTERPRETATION: 1-2 SAMUEL AND 1-2 KINGS

In these books, we find a complete story. They resemble the final stage of a family history, after the gathering of the data and the retelling of stories have all been joined together. The books of Samuel and Kings include collections of written and oral traditions, combinations of stories and legends. These materials have been reshaped in accord with contemporary needs and the spiritual horizons of their composers. Many smaller stories have been combined to form larger sections of narratives. We can often recognize them because they focus on a particular institution, person, or notion of God. Other sections, however, stand out because of their unique style of language and theology:

sometimes we find stories interspersed with very "preachy" or hortatory sections, just as family narratives occasionally turn into sermonettes. Our attentive listening to such stories, even biblical stories, will allow us to hear the differences.

The books of Samuel and Kings, then, consist of narratives which retell Israel's monarchic history. Often the stories tell more about monarchs and prophets than about ordinary people. The careful listener will, in addition, discern sections which appear to sermonize on the events of history, explaining God's role and exhorting the people to live up to their covenant obligations. Often these stories are very ancient, as in family history. Their interpretations, however, come from a later time—when the story was retold for the final time before it was set in written form. Just as family history takes on new meaning with each generation which retells it, so the biblical history attracted further nuances in later centuries while it was still being reformulated and retold in Israel.

With this in mind, the way these stories are retold, even the order in which they appear, often points clearly to later problems and interests. Through the years, historical memory deepens the insight of the work; in a similar fashion, the spiritual vision of the narratives also becomes clearer. It is possible to trace the process of literary growth in these biblical books. Such a process helps us to discern the ancient stories in the books and to separate them from later interpretations. In general, we find that history-like stories or narratives were often written near the time of the events which they describe. An example would be the history of David's court in Jerusalem, found in 2 Samuel 9-20. The larger history of the era, however, took shape later. A detailed outline of the literary development of the books of Samuel and Kings appears in Appendix II.

The Deuteronomic History

In the Jewish canon of the Scriptures the books of Samuel and Kings have always stood with Joshua and Judges in a major division of the Hebrew Bible called the Former Prophets. In similar fashion, many biblical scholars have recognized a genuine affinity between these "history" books— Joshua, Judges, 1-2 Samuel, 1-2 Kings—and the Book of Deuteronomy. Deuteronomy is usually grouped with the books of Genesis, Exodus, Leviticus, and Numbers (together the five are called the Pentateuch by scholars, or Torah in Jewish tradition). Still, Deuteronomy seems closer to the books which come after it in the biblical canon. It shares vocabulary and theological perspective with them. This distinctive view of life has led scholars to call this whole collection of writings the Deuteronomic History. This title combines the historical character of these books with the theological flavor of Deuteronomy. An overview of the contents and biblical texts of the Deuteronomic History may be found in Appendix III.

Even if one imagines this huge history as a single work, it does not necessarily follow that a single person authored it in its entirety. Rather we assume a final group of writers whose theological insight and prodigious labor shaped these books as we now know them. There is good evidence that the present version of these books comes from the time of the Exile to Babylon, when people were searching for an explanation for their catastrophe. Many biblical scholars, however, believe that the bulk of this history was composed before the final destruction of Jerusalem. Perhaps it occurred around the time of King Josiah (ca. 622 BCE), who strove to reform worship and political life of the southern kingdom of Judah. At this time a group of preachers and teachers tried to call their brothers and sisters to reform their lives, promising salvation for those who obey the Torah. It is possible that the Book of Deuteronomy came to light during these years (cf 2 Kings 22, and the discussion of Huldah the Prophetess in Chapter Six). For these reasons, scholars call these preachers and teachers the Deuteronomists, and I will use this term throughout the book.

When I speak of deuteronomic interpretation and history, I generally refer to their vision and religious program. This is discovered by studying the way in which they retold and interpreted older stories—some of which dated even to the reigns of David and Solomon. In the view of these Deuteronomists, King Josiah manifested right conduct with regard to the temple, its worship, Torah, and its relationship to prophecy. Thus he provides an excellent model of the true deuteronomic king. The style of Deuteronomy sounds like a sermon Moses preached before Israel entered the `Promise Land. This homiletic style of speaking characterizes much of the books of Samuel and Kings, so we may consider deuteronomic language as key to a preaching spirituality especially suited to the seventh century.

There are deuteronomic sermons, homilies, and theological reflection pieces in 1 Samuel 12, 1 Kings 8 and 2 Kings 17. They can be identified because they share the distinctive language and spiritual vision of the Book of Deuteronomy.

Once these passages become familiar to a reader, many shorter passages and even brief comments fall into a similar pattern of stylized language and similar theology. This process resembles our listening to the sermonette by Gregory the Great; once we understand the style of his own homiletic comment on the story, we could more easily pinpoint his interpretive comments in his other writings. I have used these criteria in the books of Samuel and Kings to discern deuteronomic passages. Then I can reflect on these passages as these authors' interpretations of the ancient story. Those passages which appear to come from the Deuteronomists provide an important witness to homiletic spirituality in ancient Israel.

BIBLICAL STORY AND INTERPRETATION: 1-2 CHRONICLES

The author of 1-2 Chronicles also presents a history-type writing for his audience. These books contain several kinds of source materials: genealogies, historical narratives, prayers, and sermons. We will read these books as we read the Deuteronomic History. The way in which the author understands and presents the materials remains our prime interest since it suggests how the sources were appreciated and evaluated. Then we can begin to discern the goals and intentions of the author. Comparison between a traditional source [1-2 Samuel, 1-2 Kings] and its presentation in 1-2 Chronicles offers an excellent way of understanding the interpretation offered in these books.

The Chronicler's History

The author of 1-2 Chronicles often follows the narrative of Samuel and Kings very closely. This helps us to identify the source easily and to make comparative studies. When we notice even slight variations between the story in Chronicles and the books of Samuel and Kings, we have found this author's view of the older story.

A particular example of this would be the following. After David's entry into Jerusalem, Hiram the king of Tyre sent him massive amounts of building materials. When the writer of 2 Samuel mentions that David's family increased greatly in numbers, he implies a connection between house construction and family size. But the text in 1 Chronicles differs slightly.

2 Samuel 5	1 Chronicles 14
[13] And David took *more concubines and* wives	[3] And David took more wives
from Jerusalem	in Jerusalem,
after he came from Hebron;	and
and more sons and more daughters were born to David.	David begot more sons and daughters.

The following verse in each book names the children born to David in Jerusalem. The Chronicler gives two more names than 2 Samuel, though he did not mention David's concubines. Perhaps the Chronicler was more concerned to give a complete, accurate list. He also tried to protect David's character from being tarnished by neglecting to mention his concubines.

The Chronicler uses other techniques as well to retell the

older story. Sometimes the Chronicler adds names, as we noted above, and emphasizes roles and offices held by people. This is true especially for the Levites, who attain new prominence in Chronicles. So this author writes a history with a theological and homiletic touch, attempting to contemporize ancient sacred traditions for the spiritual nourishment of people of his own era and region.

This contemporizing of the biblical tradition teaches us about the Chronicler's hopes and goals. The books of 1-2 Chronicles seem to have been written in fifth or fourth century Palestine. A somewhat discouraged Jewish community lived there, since it had experienced grave difficulty reconstituting itself after its return from the Exile. The Jews experienced the political impotence of the vanquished under Persian rule, so the author tries to create for them a spiritual center and focus to help them maintain their identity and integrity.

Identity through religion was the only possibility for them, since they were politically dependent. So the temple and its personnel—priests and Levites—could provide a great rallying point for the people Israel. Although the monarchy had never reappeared after the Exile, the Chronicler rewrote the story of David (from 1-2 Samuel) in order to present him as the originator and the spiritual head of the temple and its cult. These institutions were part of Jewish life during the Chronicler's era, so he did well to connect them with King David. He reinterpreted their early history to suit present circumstances.

The Chronicler was not simply a teacher giving explanations to the Jews of his day. As a preacher, he issued a powerful exhortation to them to stand faithful to temple worship. He also encouraged the various ministers of the temple: he took the time and effort to list them by family in his genealogies, and he paid special attention to their duties and accomplishments. This was especially true for the Levites. In 1-2 Chronicles the homiletic tendencies are certainly present, portraying a spirituality to which this "preacher" was inviting post-exilic Jews in Palestine. These books offer an ancient example of spirituality well suited to the life-situation of the audience.

Spirituality and Situation in Life

In our discussion of the story of Scholastica and Benedict I spoke of spiritualities corresponding to their situations in life. We assume that Benedict's concern to return to his monastery cell arose not from selfish motives but from his monastic values. We have no reason to presume that the way of life which had nourished him so long was at fault. From the viewpoint of his monastic spirituality, Benedict's response is quite correct. His first response coheres nicely with the values of his social and religious institutional setting.

Scholastica's request and prayer for more time in conversation with her brother was more difficult to explain. She also lived a monastic life in a community of women, and we have no reason to suspect that her community followed a way of life much different from her brother's. For that reason, her response puzzles us. If we ascribe to her the same basic religious values which guided her brother, her persistence in following her own desire seems quite out of character. Perhaps her actions reveal her own personality and beliefs as much as her situation in life. Scholastica's action alerts us to the fallibility of explaining everything in terms of life setting.

Finally, Gregory's use of a story about Benedict would not initially surprise us, since he may have been a monk before he was elected pope. What does surprise us is his telling of a story which does not cast the traditional hero in the best light! But Gregory's new interpretation of the story reflects his new stance in life. As bishop of Rome he had pastoral responsibility for the entire church, not just those of one group or one region. His reflection on the expression from the Gospel of John broadens the scope of the story. He asserts that God is love, that the one who loves more accomplishes more. All Christians can live out this spiritual vision. Of course, not everyone can draw practical conclusions from his words. Some who are inspired by his message of love might decide to pursue monastic life as a way to live out this spirituality. Now we have come full circle!

One's situation in life does make a difference, even if it cannot explain everything we do. In contemporary speech we say that social setting powerfully influences one's life, even though we deny its ultimate power to determine what one does. Even so, the uniqueness of our ways of life stands out the more clearly when seen against the backdrop of our social and religious settings. Whenever someone follows an unexpected path we take notice of his or her individual personality. We ponder Scholastica's personality and spirituality precisely because she does what we would not expect.

We in the twentieth century experience a great variety of alternative spiritualities presented for our choice. We also realize that our own freedom to choose depends on many factors, including the familial and cultural situation into which we have been born, as well as the nurture and education we received. Our range of choice largely coheres with our vision of the world. Realities like the structure and beliefs of our church radically affect the way we look at the world and our own role in it.

Since my own options are both restricted and encouraged by those institutions in which I am embedded, a focus on Israel's major institutions during the era of the monarchy could lead us to the spiritualities of these biblical books. For this reason, one way of organizing my quest for spirituality in these books kept recurring to me: major social and religious institutions of Israel. There our ancestors in faith found meaning, identity, and relationship with God. As I pondered the books of Samuel, Kings, and Chronicles, I became more convinced that their original audiences experienced God's call to full life not only through the temple and the prophets of those times, but also through the spiritual leadership provided by the monarchy. Each grasps an aspect of truth, though none exhausts it.

Israel's institutions can help us to grasp resources for our own life and spirituality. Each of them—monarchy, temple, word of God—represents a social and religious institution or group in Israel. Those who are most closely involved with each setting find there a unique way of experiencing God and the human community. As we contemplate each of these institutions, however, we focus not only on that phenomenon—e.g., the reigning monarch, the temple as building, a particular prophet—but also on the entire culture in which it is embedded. So the social, economic, religious and political sides all have a story to tell.

is concern for life setting determines my second organizing principle. In each of the chapters that follow, I attempt to discern the spirituality of an institution or life setting in Israel by focusing on a few narratives or texts which speak to our concerns. I choose this method of presentation because it seems a helpful way to relate these biblical texts with real-life settings, where they might provide resources for our own spirituality. I hope that some of these "close readings" will spark questions for you and suggest ways of reading other texts on your own.

The three parts of this book correspond to the three main spiritualities of these biblical books, Monarchy, Temple, and Word of God. I will devote two chapters to each institution. For each institution, the first chapter will concentrate on narrative sources of that spirituality. This narrative spirituality usually comes from older writers and scribes who told these stories at times close to the events. The second chapter on each institution will treat the homiletic spirituality of the Deuteronomists and the Chronicler. As we reflect on each of these spiritualities we may find distinct ways of living, believing, hoping and praying appropriate to our own changing situations. If these biblical texts belong to all of us, then perhaps each of us can find in them a home.

PART I

The Monarchy

For more than four centuries, Israel existed as a people administered by a monarchic form of government. After the era of settlement of the Land described in the Book of Joshua, more than a century followed in which the various Hebrew tribes coexisted in the land of Canaan. The Book of Judges describes some aspects of Israelite life during this period, focusing on the growing threat posed by the Philistine peoples and the feats of the great charismatic "judges" who saved Israel from external enemies. Then came Saul, anointed "prince" of the people by the prophet Samuel around 1020 BCE. Brought on by the need to resist Philistine advances, the loosely confederated tribes now achieved a form of political and religious unity under their leader from the tribe of Benjamin.

This form of government developed through the rule of David (1000-961 BCE), who became king of both the southern and northern tribes and effected their unity when he established Jerusalem as his capital. Solomon accelerated programs of his father and made Israel a political force in the region. After his death, Jeroboam and Rehoboam split the kingdom (922 BCE) and from that time two monarchs ruled the separated kingdoms of Israel in the North and Judah in the South. Monarchy in the northern realm ended with the Assyrian invasion of 722 BCE; in the southern kingdom, it lasted until the destruction of Jerusalem by Babylon in 587 BCE and the exile of many of Judah's elite citizens to Babylon. Monarchy lasted from 1020 until 587 BCE as the form of political administration in Israel.

If we focus on the monarchs themselves, we find them fulfilling a variety of functions during their reigns. For our purposes, we may speak of three different types of royal activity in Israel: military, legal, and religious. Defense of the country and its people occupied much of the time and energy of the kings, and it often combined with astute initiatives in the area of international policies and relations. This aspect of their lives is the subject of political and military histories of Israel which rely heavily on the narratives in Samuel and Kings. Kings or monarchs also had ultimate responsibility for the quest for justice within their realms and they occasionally adjudicated legal cases and disputes among their people. Israel's monarchs shared with their regional neighbors a view of the monarch's responsibility to support the rights of the poor, especially widows and orphans. The rulers' obligation to further the *shalom*, the well-being of the whole people emerges from study of certain Psalms (e.g. Ps 72) and from comparison with texts coming from Israel's neighbors.

These rulers also attended to the religious institutions in their realm, providing for construction, maintenance and worship, especially at the Jerusalem temple. In the earlier years of the monarchy, David and Solomon occasionally fulfilled specific roles in Israel's worship at the site of the Temple. In a parallel development, the kingship also took on a religious meaning, so that the king was considered to be God's son (Ps 2:7), firstborn of God (Ps 89:27), who established divine justice in the world (Ps 45:4, 7; Ps 72:1-4). David considered the life of Saul so sacred that he could do him no harm (1 Sam 24:6; 26:9). After the covenant with David (2 Sam 7), God's intimate relationship with descendants of this line offered religious contact with God.

These features of the king's life provide a starting point for discerning the spirituality of the monarch in Israel. These biblical books, especially 1-2 Samuel, provide a wealth of narrative evidence for determining how the king lived, what he valued and how he saw his relationship to the people and to God. This is especially true for David. For example, the tradition of God's everlasting covenant with David [2 Sam 7] provides rich resources for those who lack the resilience to live faithfully in time of trouble and despair. At times of hardship and defeat the monarchy provides genuine help for living.

Surveying the other stories in these books, we can describe David's spirituality, and that of many other rulers in Israel. We can profit greatly from reflecting on their motives, hopes, values, and actions, trusting that their spirituality suggests certain values for contemporary leaders. Here we discern a spirituality of the monarch. We cannot claim however, to have described or presented a spirituality of the monarchy. Monarchy encompasses the entire people affected by the rule of the monarch. Many of those people relate very closely to their ruler, either because of their occupations and social roles, or because of their beliefs and values. Therefore a spirituality of the monarchy also encompasses the values and ways of acting of the people of the realm; we can suppose that those whose professions tied them to the king found much of their meaning and identity in their support of the monarch's role and leadership.

Certainly we could learn much from the members of the royal family, from the king's wives, children, attendants and guards. Then we could search further, wondering what motivated the master of the palace, the royal secretaries and heralds, tax gatherers and leaders of the gangs of forced laborers, the heads of administrative districts, the judges, the directors of the royal farms and lands. Each of these, and their friends and family members, would have found the institution of the monarchy a key element in their identity, motivations and choices.

I do not propose a study of the bureaucrats and all the common people who served David and his descendants, but I suggest that their witness is essential for discerning a spirituality of the monarchy. As we view the kings through the stories told about them, we will gain some access to the life and values of the subjects of the stories—the kings, their support groups, and those whose lives they affect. At the same time, we may identify our lives not only with the great and imposing figures in these biblical books, but also with the many others whose lives more closely resemble ours.

In the next two chapters I will describe some nourishment which we can draw from Israel's rule by monarchs. We, who often resist authoritarianism and all of its trappings, must struggle to enter the world of Israel which found comfort, security, and challenge in the presence of monarchic leadership. In short, I will attempt to distill from some of these narratives life-giving resources for faithful life in our own day.

Chapter One will explore two portraits of David found in the books of Samuel, with special focus on the assistance each of them could provide for its Israelite audience. Since these portrayals come from narrative texts, this chapter will present our first exercise in narrative spirituality.

In Chapter Two we will observe how the preachers and teachers of Israel developed a homiletic spirituality from some of these same texts. We will discover, for example, radically different views of Solomon within 1 Kings 3-11. Many of the critical comments derive from deuteronomic interpretation of stories. Their concern that the monarch abide by the directions of Torah provides a first example of homiletic spirituality.

After the Exile the author of Chronicles pondered the books of Samuel and Kings and then wrote another interpretation of the reigns of David and Solomon. In 1-2 Chronicles, these kings appear less interested in Israel's military and political life than they did in the Books of Samuel and Kings. The Chronicler's emphasis on the religious and liturgical duties of the ruler forms part of this second homiletic spirituality of the monarchy.

1

PORTRAITS OF KING DAVID: NARRATIVE SPIRITUALITY OF THE MONARCHY

Of all the kings of Israel, David proved most fascinating for the biblical writers. The amount of the story they devote to David exceeds by five times that accorded to Solomon, his nearest contender. Since the final editors of these books include so many stories about David, they provide an excellent place to begin this presentation of narrative spirituality.

In this chapter I will show how the monarchy, especially David's reign, grew out of the particular needs of a turbulent political and social scene in pre-monarchic times. Stories which relate his rise to power present an optimistic view of his leadership qualities. Focusing on his ability to bring about justice through compassion, they offer an exciting model for new leadership. Later stories, however, chart the troubled course of events during his later years, when passion and breach of family trust bode ill for his ability to govern well. These differing portrayals of David suggest Israel's continuing fascination with this monarch. These stories also witness to his enduring importance as a person whose life offers challenge, hope, and a mirror for many people in Israel and beyond.

Anarchy in the Book of Judges

One way to appreciate David's rise to the role of king is to survey conditions in Israel shortly before his time. What factors evoked the advent of fresh leadership among these tribes? The narratives in the Book of Judges depict life in Israel when the tribes coexisted in a loosely organized confederacy of equals. In times of military threat, charismatic leaders arose to save the tribes from their enemies; they were called "judges." Moreover, the tone established by narratives about this era can teach us what Israelites yearned for at that time. The final chapters of Judges [chapters 17-21] relate a series of devastating episodes during this era when no monarch reigned and judges seemed no longer to function. In Judges, these stories follow the colorful and popular stories about Samson [Judg 13-16]. There the narrator clearly outlines the Philistine threat to the Israelite tribes. In addition the story interweaves hints about the corrupting Philistine influence on Samson's checkered life. Israel had struggled mightily against their god Dagon, but their hero's life was snuffed out when the Philistines identified and capitalized on his personal weakness—his relationship with women. The Samson narratives are not simply the story of an individual; they also portend the deteriorating moral and social fabric of the tribes. Samson's mixture of strength and weakness indirectly symbolizes the problems faced by early Israel.

These final chapters of Judges demonstrate the developing anarchy of the waning days of tribal confederation. The stories in Judges 17-18 expose the dangers brought on by pride and possessiveness in the sphere of worship. In Judges 19-21 more horrifying tales illustrate the breakdown in social morality and intertribal relations as characteristic of this era. These narratives present faithful people of ancient and modern eras with eloquent challenges to their way of life. In addition to providing critique of early Israelite behavior (with which we might find contemporary connections), they also emphasize the desire for change in the pattern of leadership in Israel.

A contemporary situation in our judicial sphere illustrates both of these tendencies, of societal critique and agitation for change. Our legal system has fallen prey to innumerable ways to subvert justice for capital crimes. This situation invites just criticism and leads to a clamoring for institutional change. For example, frustration mounts because of the difficulty of removing dangerous criminals from society through life imprisonment. This leads many to demand the more radical solution of the death sentence. In a similar fashion the stories of Judges 17-21 aim to persuade an audience of the need for social and institutional change in early Israel. These stories in Judges suggest similar challenges for those who pursue social reform today.

Dishonest Levites [Judges 17-18]

Immediately after the Samson story, the narrative describes abuses in worship. A young man in the hill country of Ephraim, Micah, capitalized on his mother's recovery of lost money to build and equip for her a house shrine for

Yahwistic worship [Judg 17:1-6]. Then the storyteller interrupts the story: "In those days there was no king in Israel; every man did what was right in his own eyes" [Judg 17:6]. Does the commentator disapprove of this cultic arrangement, the house shrine? One detail of the story refutes this interpretation: the money he used was part of what he had stolen from his mother [Judg 17:2]. This shrine stands on the foundation of ill-gotten gain—hardly an auspicious portent for its future. Only in the seventh century BCE, after the deuteronomic crusade to centralize worship in the Jerusalem temple [Deut 12], would the existence of local shrines like this one become a problem.

Another worship problem emerges from this story. The desire for personalization and localization of worship—like the local shrine of Micah—runs the risk of catering to purely personal purposes. While this story does not necessarily speak against popular piety and household prayer, it does pose questions for those who might wish to replace communal worship on a larger scale by gatherings in more intimate settings. In recent years, for example, some religious communities have asked themselves if their practice of daily Eucharist in their own houses fosters integration into the local church or makes it more difficult.

The second episode in the hills of Ephraim concerns the personnel for this shrine. Although Micah had first relied on one of his sons to serve as priest [Judg 17:5], he later seized the opportunity to hire a wandering Levite to replace him [Judg 17:7-13]. Micah's motivation seems no better than before; he said, "Now I know that the LORD will prosper me, because I have a Levite as priest" [Judg 17:13]. One wonders what will result from his desire to invest his shrine with a priest who has status (Levitical) and who will be reliable because he receives wages.

Micah's Levitical priest raises issues for our own practice of ministry today, as well as our valuation of pastors. Does social and religious status or lengthy tenure count for more than the proclamation of the word? The desire for success, power, and prestige exerts strong pulls on religious leaders. This Levite subtly challenges us to reexamine our own concepts of ministry.

In Judges 18 the story returns to the tribe of Dan (Samson's tribe) as it searched for territory on the northern borders of the country. Enroute they pass through Ephraim and consult Micah's priest about their prospective attack on the Canaanite settlement of Laish. Later they return to buy off this Levite and his cultic images for their own worship needs. Finally they install him at a sanctuary they erected on the site of the conquered town of Laish, which they named Dan [Judg 18:29-31].

This story explains how the tribe of Dan ended up in the far north of the land, but also contains inauspicious hints about the future. First, Dan's shrine was established by a Levite who had severed his relations with Micah, who had treated him "like one of his sons" [Judg 17:11]. This tribe's priest was one who had chosen a better financial offer. Second, the people whom the Danites had destroyed at Laish are described in positive terms.

Judges 18
[7] Then the five men departed, and came to Laish, and saw the people who were there, how they dwelt in security, after the manner of the Sidonians, quiet and unsuspecting, lacking nothing that is in the earth, and possessing wealth, and how

> they were far from the Sidonians and had no dealings with anyone.

These were qualities which the Danites could have emulated. Perhaps an editor left a positive description of the conquered people here in the text as a comment about Dan's actions. Some indigenous peoples deserved imitation rather than destruction. The story of Micah demonstrates how abuses in the tribal worship life tainted their entire societal structure and ethos and led them to desire more effective leadership. This yearning for reform appears again in the formula which introduced this story about the Danites: "In those days there was no king in Israel" [Judg 18:1].

If such a discordant note in the biblical text can pique our interest about Israel's life, we might also allow it to invite our hearing of many dissonant voices in our own society. The voice of dissent about treatment of Native Americans in the United States was largely silenced in popular American history until recent decades. Just as the biblical editor spoke only with difficulty, many contemporary critics discover that they must speak with subtlety as well as courage.

Rape and Its Consequences [Judges 19-24]

The destructiveness of intertribal conflicts progressively increased in early Israel. In the narratives of Judges 19-21 they derive largely from abominable sexual behavior. First, the narrator recounts the horrifying crime of the Benjaminite men, who ravished and raped to death the concubine of a Levite from Ephraim [Judges 19]. Notice how this narrator introduces the terrible account: "In those days, when there was no king in Israel" [Judg 19:1]. This commentator does not account for the evil actions, but he struggles to explain the powerlessness of the other tribes to persuade the tribe of Benjamin to hand over its few guilty members [Judg 20:12-13].

These stories would appear quite differently through the lens of the female characters. The Levite's concubine suffered inhuman outrage when she was calmly offered to the "base young men" in place of the Levite whom they had first hoped to abuse sexually [Judg 19:25]. What worth had she? What hospitality code could spare the man while yielding the woman to such violence? Paradoxically, this is the same woman who previously had become "angry with him [the Levite], and . . . went away from him to her father's house at Bethlehem in Judah" [Judg 19:2]. When her husband came for her, he arrived armed only with words: "he went after her, to speak kindly to her and bring her back"[Judg 19:3]. In a world where only men had the prerogative for divorce [Deut 24:1-4] her bold act stands out for all to ponder: what was the source of her courage?

Yet she remains in the male world of the narrative. It never reports a single word of dialogue in which she speaks. Her husband's plan to speak kindly with her became a reconciliatory speech with her father. During the journey the Levite spoke with his servant and the old man who met them in Gibeah. He never said a word to her. After these kinds of insensitive behavior, the atrocities which follow— she was raped until dead and her body hacked up into twelve pieces as evidence of the abomination for the other tribes—do not prove shocking, for the sensitivities of the hearers have already been dulled. But other women would have been terrified by the possible implications for them-

selves. What would prevent them from facing similar
violence? They might also have been mystified by the
sudden change in attitudes, since Samson had dealt much
more mutually with the women in his life. What has led to
the devaluation of women that marks the passage from the
Samson stories to the next set?

These sobering questions cannot be avoided, even if we
can find no easy answers. These tribes manifested contradictory values as they dealt with their women. The
dignity accorded them in one cycle of stories is nullified by
the brutalities of Judges 19-21. If a woman's life has no
worth in one situation, how can men be trusted in another?
A feminist perspective on these stories not only adds to our
understanding of women's roles and status in early Israel, but
it also provides a different and seldom heard voice, reminding
us that the brutalizing of any person or group ultimately
affects all. The violation of this concubine portends violence
for all, and the women intuitively know that, even when
their voice is neither sought nor heard.

Similar questions arise today concerning sexual violence
and harassment as the effects of misogynism on our social
and moral fabric. Can we expect to heal our society's ills or
the problems faced within our churches if we concurrently
ignore these forms of indignity? Can we answer today that
question the women in Gibeah might have posed? What do
the Near Eastern hospitality codes mean in face of this
atrocity? How can men speak of peace without working to
achieve reconciliation between women and men? How can a
church describe the economic injustices of American
capitalism without facing the economic marginalization of
many of its own women? These are some persistent
questions posed by women.

The nameless, battered concubine of Judges 19 has a life today if she finally finds hearers for her voice of agony, an agony she shares with other women, with all who are brutalized. Passion for change remains as keen in our day as at the end of the era of the Judges.

Returning to Israel, we find all the tribes but Benjamin gathered at Mizpah in order to deal with the atrocity in Gibeah [Judg 20:1-13]. They send to the Benjaminites an urgent request to hand over the guilty men in order to eradicate the evil.

> *Judges 20*
> [12] And the tribes of Israel sent men through all the tribe of Benjamin, saying, "What wickedness is this that has taken place among you? [13] Now therefore give up the men, the base fellows in Gibeah, that we may put them to death, and put away evil from Israel." But the Benjaminites would not listen to the voice of their brethren, the people of Israel.

There is tremendous pathos in the air when the narrator concludes that Benjamin would not "listen to the voice" of those who had experienced the evil. Listening to the voice of the wronged is what God has done for Israel and what Israelites should do for each other. Benjamin's refusal to hear the cry of the wronged defines the depth of evil in this episode.

We should not be surprised, however, by Benjamin's departure from Israelite covenantal faith: people who do not listen to the voice of a battered, dying woman would not be expected to respond to the word of their accuser. Tribes which do not harken to the voice of the oppressed do not deserve to be part of Israel. Only after Benjamin's refusal do the other tribes join forces to take action against them [Judg

20:14-48]. Benjamin's behavior also emphasizes similar deafness among members of the other tribes, including the Levite who harkened to his concubine's voice only after she had angrily deserted him. Israel requires not only a king; it also needs prophets who will articulate God's word about the cries of the wronged.

The narrator of Judges 17-21 clearly wished to demonstrate both the character of these tribes which shared a common covenantal relationship with their God and the deterioration of Israelite society when it lacked effective leadership. When each person did what he or she considered upright, the results were appalling [Judg 21:25, repeating 17:6]. The final editor repeats four times a formula which summarizes the overall problem: "In those days there was no king in Israel" [Judg 17:6; 18:1; 19:1; 21:25]. This terse analysis of Israel's atrocities in Judges 17-21 points clearly to the need for new leadership. This yearning would culminate in Israel's insistence with Samuel: "appoint for us a king to govern us like all the nations" [1 Sam 8:5].

David as Deliverer from Anarchy

Although Saul became Israel's first king, he did not fully accomplish the transition to a new style of political order. Very early in his career, the young David appeared on the scene and began to serve him and outshine him. David may not have been Israel's first king, but he initiated a thorough transformation from struggling tribes to monarchy.

The stories about David exhibit several theological messages and sociological concerns, so we may speak of different "portraits" of David.[4] The remaining sections of this chapter will focus on two portraits of David which emerge from the biblical story. We will treat the optimistic story of David's rise [1 Sam 16—2 Sam 5], and the story of David's court [2 Sam 9-20 and 1 Kgs 1-2]. Each of these "stories" about David attempts to describe his life and deeds in a picturesque fashion, but they also suggest a religious viewpoint from which to understand David's role in Israel's history.

For our interests, however, this variety of portraits can pose important questions. Which portrayal appeals most to us? Which best characterizes the church or ecclesial community with which we identify? Which would best express the social and political goals to which we subscribe? As we ponder questions like these we can also return to the biblical stories with a new lens and begin to identify the theological and anthropological presuppositions which we hold. We might also subject them to friendly criticism.

DAVID'S RISE AND TRIBAL OPTIMISM
[1 Sam 16:14—2 Sam 5:10]

In the story of David's rise [1 Sam 16:14—2 Sam 5:10], for example, the narrator wishes us to understand that

---

[4]Of particular interest is Walter Brueggemann's study of David, *David's Truth in Israel's Imagination and Memory* (Philadelphia: Fortress, 1984). Since his questons are not historical, but focus on how Israel imagined and remembered David as a "resource for faithful living" [p. 111], they easily suggest questions of genuine significance for biblical spirituality today: how can these traditions provide us with imaginative memories of relationship with God which aids us in our attempts to live faithfully and with steadfast love?

David's rise to power and authority was no mere political event, but harpened according to the directives and guidance of God. The end of this section contains a theological comment: "And David became greater and greater, for the LORD, the God of hosts, was with him" [2 Sam 5:10]. This comment also expresses the story's mood.

The tradition contained many stories about David's youth and his battles against the Philistines [1 Sam 17]; his flight from Saul [1 Sam 19-22]; his relationship with Saul's son, Jonathan [1 Sam 19-20]; his sparing of Saul's life [1 Sam 24, 26]; and his wanderings in the Judean desert [1 Sam 27-30]. Some of these stories relate incidents that could prove less flattering and edifying than the narrator would have wished. When we receive them from the storyteller, the disturbing questions about David's character are unlikely to arise. As we hear the story, it cleverly defends David against charges that he ruthlessly pursued a path of political machinations on his way to royal power. Our narrator achieves this almost without comment. The story proceeds in such a way that we can identify the important points in David's life and make our own judgments about the way he behaved.

These stories, then, present David rising to power in spite of all odds, particularly Saul's murderous hatred. The literary portrait of David in 1 Sam 16—as slight, young, attractive— does provide a symbolic suggestion that David rose to royal leadership from a position of relative unimportance. When Saul sought a lyre player to deliver him from the torments of his "evil spirit" [1 Sam 16:14], the king's young servant reported seeing a certain "son of Jesse, a Bethlehemite, who is skilful in playing, a man of valor, prudent in speech, and a man of good presence; and the LORD is with him" [1 Sam

16:18]. This points baldly to God's favor toward David, and it forms the perfect counterpart to his ordinary origins in Bethlehem.

Yet David's rise does not appear as some kind of miracle, for it occurs through the course of ordinary events. "David came to Saul and entered his service. And Saul loved him greatly, and he became his armor-bearer" [1 Sam 16:21]. God's care for David became evident only through his success in the human situation. After reflection, an editor recognized God's action in David's rise, adding the theological finale "the LORD is with him."

This story artfully illustrates young David's general excellence and his support for the troubled King Saul. Such a view of David implicitly offers hope and a sense of self-worth to those who support the young monarch. Insignificance can be transformed! There is yet hope for the lowly, for those who live at the fringes of society, symbolized by the picture of David wandering through the southern Judean desert region.

This rise to power also includes transformation of Israelite society. It marks the transition from the anarchy of the tribal confederation to justice, order, and stability under the monarchy. David's personal fate effects a marvelous transition in Israel; it also promises similar transformation for all who supported him. For all who come at later times, David's rise offers hope for success against all reasonable odds, if the LORD accompanies them. To those who struggle today to bring justice and order to frayed social structures, David's example proclaims that power for good need not come from those who appear strong and inspire awe.

Abigail and David [1 Samuel 25]

Many vivid narratives comprise this picture of David's rise, but I would like to focus on the story of Abigail and Nabal [1 Sam 25:2-42]. It is not central to the illustration of David's development, but it does suggest a connection between his leadership ability and his dealings with people. Featuring as protagonist a woman of significance (unlike the muted and unnamed woman of Judges 19) this story introduces us to the first person to acclaim David as prince (*nagid*).

David and his traveling band provide protective service for Nabal's flocks and shepherds, so David expects recompense from this sheep farmer during the festival of the sheep shearing. David sends ten of his young men to request hospitality and supplies from Nabal (whose name means "fool"). When he hears their petition, Nabal insults their leader by asking "Who is David? Who is the son of Jesse?" [1 Sam 25:10]. After hearing this news from his young men, David prepares them for reprisals against Nabal [1 Sam 25:13].

At the same time, a second drama develops in Nabal's camp. One young man reports the whole interchange to Abigail, Nabal's wife, who is a woman "of good understanding and beauty" [1 Sam 25:3]. She quickly grasps the danger posed by David's anger, which the narrator also reports.

1 Samuel 25
[21] Now David had said, "Surely in vain have I guarded all that this fellow has in the wilderness, so that nothing was missed of all that belonged to him; and he has returned me evil for good. [22] God do so to David and more also, if by

morning I leave so much as one male of all who belong to him."

Alarmed by the possibility of attack, Abigail devises a bold plan to honor David's request and to seek reconciliation with him. She personally sends gifts of food to appease David and his band.

David's resort to violence comes as a surprise after he had spared Saul's life in the previous chapter [1 Sam 24]. In contrast to his restraint with regard to Saul, David proposes vengeance against Nabal. It seems strange that he would kill Nabal, who had only insulted him, after refusing to harm Saul, who had attempted to kill him. Could his respect for the king run so deeply? Could it project to a hope for his own reign?

Then Abigail encounters David as he comes to battle [1 Sam 25:23-35]. She does obeisance to David and suggests that all the blame should rest on her, since she was not aware of the mission of David's messengers. She makes excuses for her husband, Nabal, "for as his name is, so is he" [v.25]. Although the name means "fool", she renders the term as "ill-natured" [v.25], subtly indicating that "folly is with him." She delicately avoids outright ridicule of her husband and refrains from mentioning her real motive for staying David's retribution: she wants something from him. She also displays the theological prowess which results from her wisdom. To restrain David's violence in this situation would mean that the LORD protects David from bloodguilt [1 Sam 25:26]. Thus she offers the hospitality which Nabal should have given.

Her clever defense works, and Nabal's life is spared and David's integrity is preserved. Ten days later, however, her husband dies of natural causes when "the LORD smote Nabal and he died" [v.38]. David becomes the focus of the story again, as he responds to her request.

> *1 Samuel 25*
> [32] Blessed be the LORD, the God of Israel, who sent you this day to meet me! [33] Blessed be your discretion, and blessed be you, who have kept me this day from bloodguilt and from avenging myself with my own hand! [34] For as surely as the LORD the God of Israel lives, who has restrained me from hurting you, unless you had made haste and come to meet me, truly by morning there had not been left to Nabal as much as one male.

David cannot decide whether Abigail [33] or the LORD [34] held him back from unnecessary violence. Perhaps this narrator wants the audience to realize that her clever wisdom and beauty embody both God's gift and protection for David. To his credit, David does not quibble about its source.

Abigail accomplishes much without flamboyance of any kind. She responds to David as a true Israelite should; her positive response to him symbolizes her wisdom, and sets her off from the folly of her husband's insult to him. She also restrains David from unnecessary violence, from actions characteristic of the era of the Judges which had threatened to reemerge in Saul's murderous chase after David. Her actions help to lead David from anarchy to order and justice.

The narrator views Abigail as preparing David for his role as prince (*nagid*) and as king. Her words have begun the process of reversing the injustice suffered by her silent and unnamed sister, the concubine from Bethlehem [Judges 19]. She embodies a care for preservation of human life that pierces through the impassioned retributive design of David. She exercises the craft and irony of the ancient Hebrew midwives [Exod 1:17] who had preserved human life from Pharaoh's violence. Although she has accomplished this without explicit word from the LORD, the storyteller recognizes her actions as effecting God's designs. Her wisdom has the power to evoke from David new ways of behavior in accord with prudence and justice, so she contributes to the social transformation implied by Israel's yearning for a king.

Finally, Abigail seems to possess king-making powers. She is the first person to call him prince (*nagid*).

> *1 Samuel 25*
>
> [28] Pray forgive the trespass of your handmaid; for the LORD will certainly make my lord a sure house, because my lord is fighting the battles of the LORD; and evil shall not be found in you so long as you live. [29] If men rise up to pursue you and to seek your life, the life of my lord shall be bound in the bundle of the living in the care of the LORD your God . . . [30] And when the LORD has done to my lord according to all the good that he has spoken concerning you, and has appointed you prince (*nagid*) over Israel, [31] my lord shall have no cause of grief, or pangs of conscience, for having shed blood without cause or for my lord taking vengeance himself. And when the LORD has dealt well with my lord, then remember your handmaid."

Effectively, she proclaims David as king, since she assures him of the same "princely" status accorded to Saul by Samuel [1 Sam 9:16; 10:1]. Moreover, she preempts Nathan's oracle in 2 Samuel 7 by promising David a "sure house" [v.28] even before David meets the royal prophet in Jerusalem. Finally, she emphasizes the role of the LORD in all this, doing "according to all the good that he has spoken concerning you" [v.30].

Since Abigail's proclamation prepares for the Nathan oracle, we might suggest that a prophet was not always required for the speaking of God's wisdom. The wise person makes a significant and parallel contribution. While David's reign provides hope for the marginated and downtrodden, Abigail's wisdom and cunning offer dignity and opportunity to women and others who were regularly subordinated. In more ways than we first realized, this story of Abigail and David offers hope for future contributions by all those who belong to Israel's tribes. Abigail manifests an access to the monarch and an impact on him which could raise the spirits of other women. For women of her day she models a challenging style of relating to her (soon to be) husband. David, by contrast, experiences the salvific restraint of this woman and hears God's word spoken through her. His example opens possibilities for other men to find similar opportunities during their lives.

Abigail's encounter with David challenges some contemporary and religious stereotypes. The mixture of cunning, craft, and luck with which she fostered God's design might surprise those who search for clear moral guidelines. David wondered who had restrained his violence—God or Abigail [1 Sam 25:32ff]; his uncertainty cautions us against dogmatism about knowledge of God's will in our lives. Abigail's role in preventing a bloodbath signals the importance of activity aimed at reduction of violence and vengeance. David's willingness to be led by Abigail invites all to respond graciously, faithfully, and with trust to the wise initiatives of others, regardless of their status. This story offers a model of effective interaction between leaders and the individuals and groups who support them. Abigail persuades David to reject violence and preserve life and so helps to develop the ethos and values of the Davidic monarchy. Her example invites faithful people today to use their wit, wisdom, and cunning to help shape the moral and social fabric of their own countries.

Some people would esteem Abigail less because her efforts ultimately gained her a new and more attractive husband. Should we question her motivation and accuse her of conniving, instead of congratulating her for wisdom and discretion in these matters? Perhaps this storyteller smiles at pious seriousness, suggesting that prudence need not settle for righteousness as its only reward. Rather, we find here another woman's story about saving and gaining life. As the midwives in Egypt gained families on account of their courage, this woman achieves new identity and fame even to our day. Abigail's intervention subtly invites reflection on these less obvious ways of enhancing and directing leadership in our own day. In this way she not only helped the monarch to develop his own spirituality, she also demonstrated a spirituality for those who surround and support the monarch.

The story of David's rise, as we have seen, presents a tribal truth about David, where truth is not facticity in an historical sense but something claimed or asserted. This cycle of narratives presents a David who came from ignominious origins, who melded together outcast groups of Saul's reign, and who offered them possibilities of political organization and order. To participate in David's truth does not require prestige, possessions, or traditional kinds of power, but it does demand that one participate in David's values of respect for human life, reverence for the LORD's anointed, the openness to be taught by one like Abigail, and the ability to receive gracefully. To share in this kind of truth, one should aspire to realize the worth and dignity of each person. Marginated circles thrive on such hopes. Hope in this leader comes easily, because "the LORD was with him" constantly. Finally, his public life seems to cohere with his private dealings, so he does not suffer problems from tension between the public and private spheres of his life. David's supporters put so much hope and trust in his example that they find ways to overlook his faults and to submerge them in their enthusiasm for the new vision which he brought to Israel.

David's tribal truth, his charismatic success by God's hand, certainly finds counterparts today. Without specifying leaders who relate thus to their peoples, we can focus on situations of margination and powerlessness, where people yearn for change and justice, where equality in the group or society would satisfy a deep hunger, where a spirited leader can provide a living symbol of what people aspire to. Sometimes we might be tempted to look askance at a person or group which seems too easily swayed by a flawed leader. At those moments of temptation, these narratives invite us to examine those areas of life in which we yearn to be heard, to be taken seriously. There, the tribal circles tell us, you will trust all, hope all, believe all, give all.

David's Personal Contact with Anarchy

The story of David's later life, however, seems not to trust all nor to believe all. In 2 Samuel 9-20 and 1 Kings 1-2 we read stories of the reign of David after he had concentrated all the power of the kingdoms of Judah and Israel in his royal capital in Jerusalem. Here a very different picture of King David emerges. The storyteller presents a running account of the public, personal, and familial events of David's reign. These chapters emphasize the difficult choices and actions of David and his children, relatives, and officials. David's sexual appetite and crass disregard for marital fidelity in the Bathsheba affair lead to the murder of Uriah [2 Sam 11]. Yet this behavior stands in tension with the concrete fidelity which he showed to his deceased friend Jonathan when he kept fidelity with his friend's son, Mephibosheth [2 Sam 9]. These stories do not stand in isolation: they can only be understood together, as contradictory strains of the same personality.

By the time of this narrator, David's personality no longer convinces all of his followers that his public and private worlds are congruent and in order. A profound change has already taken place in him and his public. David no longer can count on divine assistance and approval for his every action. On some occasions the LORD's anger and disapproval stands forth starkly. His followers had ceased to scurry about in wilderness regions in search of food, water, and respite from Saul's forces or from Philistines, since they now hold the positions of the Jerusalem court. David's own capacities for relating and learning seem to have changed: no longer do the reprimands which he receives lead to change and conversion beyond the present crisis. For example, Nathan's parable in 2 Samuel 12 results in ad hoc repentance, but seems not to extend to the situation of a real daughter raped and discarded in the very next chapter. We turn now to the cycle of stories in which David's deeply flawed humanity shines forth.

Nathan and David [2 Samuel 12]

Many of these narratives invite serious and penetrating reflection, but I have chosen Nathan's reproach of David [2 Sam 12:1-25] as a pivotal story in the history of David's court. Following the Bathsheba union after Uriah's death, the story begins with Nathan's parable to David about the rich man and the poor man [2 Sam 12:1-7a]. It continues with the prophet's oracle of judgment against the guilty king [2 Sam 12:7b-15]. The section then concludes with the poignant scene of the death of Bathsheba and David's child stricken by the LORD [2 Sam 12:16-25]. We will consider not only the message of these stories but also their relation to other narratives in the court history. Their interconnectedness suggests for us a deeper appreciation of the interdependence between persons and events in our own lives.

After David's double crime—adultery with Bathsheba and murder of her husband Uriah—they married and she bore a son [2 Sam 11]. Then comes a theological judgment on the king's actions: "But the thing that David had done displeased the LORD" [1 Sam 11:27b]. So the LORD then "sent Nathan to David" [2 Sam 12:1], who went to the king and addressed him with the parable of the rich man and the poor man.

2 Samuel 12

[2] The rich man had very many flocks and herds; [3] but the poor man had nothing but one little ewe lamb, which he had bought . . . and it grew up with him and with his children; it used to eat of his morsel, and drink from his cup, and lie in his bosom, and it was like a daughter to him. [4] Now there came a traveler to the rich man, and he was unwilling to take one of his own flock or herd to prepare for the wayfarer who had come to him, but he took the poor man's lamb, and prepared it for the man who had come to him.

David's sense of justice awakens from its slumber and he suddenly remembers his origins. Angrily he replies to Nathan: "As the LORD lives, the man who has done this deserves to die . . . because he did this thing, and because he had no pity" [2 Sam 12:5b-6]. David has condemned his own action, and Nathan tells him so: "You are the man" [2 Sam 12:7a]. These famous words render judgment on David and they also redefine him: this king is a man, an ordinary human with responsibilities like others have. David's rank lack of pity immediately changes his role: without pity or compassion for those in his charge, he no longer exercises his reign in Israel.

Here begins "the painful truth of the man", as biblical scholar Walter Brueggemann has described this portrait of David.[5] Of what has he been accused? The parable speaks neither of murder nor of adultery, as one would expect. Rather, David's actions fail to demonstrate basic compassion for the needs of others whose possessions and power do not match his own. Uriah's relationship with Bathsheba could

[5]Brueggemann, David's Truth, pp. 41-65.

not withstand the power of David's craft. How could anyone continue to call him king when he shirked the most basic responsibility of a leader—care of the people? Listening to Nathan's words, David recognizes the breakdown of compassion, the failure to honor and support the relationship of the poor man with the ewe lamb which "was like a daughter to him." David's crime focuses on the relationship which he had sundered.

We pass from Nathan's condemnation ("You are the man") to the continuation of the narrative. The horror of David's crime does not diminish: "the LORD struck the child that Uriah's wife bore to David, and it became sick" [2 Sam 12:15b]. David already has begun to experience the final curse of the prophetic oracle; even after his days of lamenting for the child and fasting for its life, the child dies on the seventh day [2 Sam 12:18]. Some might view the child's death as divine retribution, but another approach suggests itself. David's lack of compassion in one relationship, that of Bathsheba and Uriah, has signaled the dying of another, this child of their union. The power and the horror of the story run deep. David's own words suffice for pathos.

The death of David and Bathsheba's child [2 Sam 12:15b-25] provides remarkable insight into David's basic values. His elders had observed the intensity of his prayer of lament during the infant's illness so that they feared his reaction when he heard of the death: "How then can we say to him the child is dead? He may do himself some harm" [2 Sam 12:18]. David observes their whispering, perceives that the reason is his child's death and simply asks them: "Is the child dead?" [2 Sam 12:19]. David listened as they answered yes.

2 Samuel 12

[20] Then David arose from the earth, and washed, and anointed himself, and changed his clothes; and he went into the house of the LORD and worshiped; he then went to his own house; and when he asked, they set food before him, and he ate."

The succession of action verbs all point toward a person prepared to meet life, and not to wallow in mourning or depression, so the elders ask him why he now behaves so differently. David's response provokes faith and also demonstrates it.

2 Samuel 12

[22] He said, "While the child was still alive, I fasted and wept; for I said, 'Who knows whether the LORD will be gracious to me, that the child may live?' [23] But now he is dead; why should I fast? Can I bring him back again? I shall go to him, but he will not return to me."

David stands alive, not paralyzed by death. His simple answer to the elders speak very simply about genuine prayer: it is directed toward life, and not toward death or mourning.

Should we therefore decide that Davidic prayer does not allow articulation of deepest feelings? Does it proscribe our mourning after death or loss of loved ones? Such reactions seem too simple. David and his storyteller focus us on the goal of all prayer—God's nurture and preservation of life in abundance. In fact, an almost buoyant realism comes from his prayer. David exhibits energy and life even while admitting that "I shall go to him," i.e. to join him in death. David's sadness does not defer his enjoyment of life, and his story invites us just as urgently to focus on life now.

David himself shifts his focus to the living as he turns toward Bathsheba, the sorrowing mother of the dead child. He "comforted his wife Bathsheba, and went in to her and lay with her; and she bore a son" [2 Sam 12:24]. His compassionate gesture toward her—strangely or ironically none was mentioned after the death of Uriah—proves fruitful, providing another child to fill the gap left by the first one's death. Throughout the story the narrator keeps a characteristic silence about Bathsheba's own feelings and thoughts. Finally, David's human qualities shine forth again, and the sharing of sadness and loss leads to re-integration and new life for both of them.

God's confirmation of their newfound love comes in the two names for the new child: David names him Solomon, playing on the word *shalom* (peace, wholeness, integrity), while Nathan relays the LORD's name, Jedidi'ah, the "beloved of the LORD" [2 Sam 12:25]. David has come full circle, from the lack of compassion on the marriage of Bathsheba and Uriah, to the renewal of pity shown to her after the death of their child; he has also moved from death to life.

For us the Nathan speech provides sobering questions about the quality of our own lives. Would we examine such situations in terms of individual justice, in terms of the oppression of women, or injustice to the poor? Often our presuppositions or ideology blur our view of the integrity of human relationships. The story challenges us to balance the multiple tensions between committed relationships and personal desires. What role does compassion play in our moral decision-making? Do we realize the loss of moral leadership resulting from loss of compassion?

The lovemaking which seemingly replaces David's mourning after the death of Bathsheba's first child also reverses some time-honored customs. We might learn from David that renewal of life results more in the manifestation of human compassion than in prayer and fasting. His tenderness and his honesty both invite us to more authentic life. Piety cannot replace love in David's life.

Tamar and Amnon [2 Samuel 13]

After Ammon fell to David's armies and the king himself had made a tardy appearance at the siege of that city [2 Sam 12:26-31], we hear the terrifying story of Tamar's rape by her half brother Amnon [2 Sam 13]. A double irony emerges here: first, that David should win victory spoils at the very site of Uriah's murder; and second, that his tender concern both for his child and his wife do not extend to this daughter when she is violated. The summary gives no hint of any action by the king: "When King David heard of all these things he was very angry" [2 Sam 13:21].

The rebellion of Absalom, Tamar's brother [2 Sam 13-20], evokes an even deeper pathos if we consider his shock that his father did nothing either to protect Tamar or to care for her after the incestuous rape. This story subtly demonstrates how the private events of David's life (i.e. his sexual desires) clearly affect both his family (Amnon, Tamar, Absalom) and his public exercise of authority in Israel. The curse initiated by his sin materializes not only in the private sphere but also in the violence, terror, and rebellion which mar the later years of his monarchy. David's public trust suffers from his private indiscretions, and the narrative irony

.n these stories subtly poses questions for all their hearers.

As we hear these narratives today we might reflect on the congruence between our own public and private lives. We cannot avoid facing the impact of our decisions on the lives of our children or of our communities. In particular, both Tamar and Uriah cry out through the centuries with their lament over the violence they experienced in the moment of lust. We should not focus solely on the implicit judgment of our own generation in these stories. We are invited also to hear the petition of the lamentor: Save us, O LORD. It is addressed to us as well.

Conclusion

King David's portrait is as human as it is heroic. His life becomes larger than life, nurturing the painful truth of the man along with the sure hope of the tribe. Our ancient ancestors' desire for monarchic rule parallels our own yearning for deliverance from the anarchy, chaos, and injustice of the world in which we live. While we might devise different types of alternative rule, we are tempted to hope for the solution from without rather than from within, for the external change instead of internal conversion within the community and the individual.

Often we are tempted to hope for all things, to put ultimate trust in a new leader or person—whether president, bishop, administrator, friend, or spouse. This parallels the tribal tendency to envision everything David did as good. Yet no human can fulfill all those expectations. David's darker moments in 2 Samuel's history of his later reign mirror for us some of the more sober patterns we might find in the chronicles and journals of our own lives. The gentle humor contained in irony, moreover, may prove more probative for us than the thundering voice of the prophet; if so, we have found in David's reign resources for a more faithful living of our own spirit-led lives.

2

DAVID AND SOLOMON
IN LATER TRADITIONS:
HOMILETIC SPIRITUALITY
OF THE MONARCHY

Hindsight often allows for greater analytical clarity about the past. This truism also holds for Israel and its Scriptures, especially the historical books. So we may expect David's later descendants to appraise his reign differently than those of the tenth century BCE, because needs and pressures, tensions and possibilities change significantly through the centuries. The preachers and teachers of later Israel reflected on narratives from the eras of David and Solomon and then retold them from their own point of view. In these later writings we may expect to find fresh perspectives, not only religious but also social and historical.

In this chapter I plan to focus on different moments of preaching in the story of Israel's monarchy and to describe some of the special features of each homily. Each of these homiletic interpretations contains a particular exhortation through which it provides nourishment for reflection and conversion even to our day. First we will focus on the

Solomon traditions in 1 Kings; I consider these older, enthusiastic narratives as the "court story of Solomon." Scribes supported by the king and deeply involved with the monarchic bureaucracy most likely did the research, sifting, and composition of these traditions. Here we will find a narrative spirituality.

Second, I will compare the hope-filled story of Solomon with the more sober analysis of the Deuteronomists. These seventh century BCE preachers recalled more than three centuries of monarchic rule—much of it troubled by error and corruption—as they recalled Solomon's story. Here we shall discern some striking differences between older narrative traditions and the deuteronomic exhortation to return to Torah and covenant.

In the third section, we will turn to the portrayal of David in the Chronicler's history. Here we meet a distinctive spirituality of the Jewish community in Palestine after it had returned from the Exile in Babylon. Lacking political autonomy, these Jews focus more energy on worship in their temple than on government service. In the Chronicler's presentation of David we meet a more liturgical view and spirituality than seen before.

Deuteronomic Spirituality of the Monarchy

Solomon's rule probably brought Israel to its most powerful and influential stage of its entire history. Such judgments, however, must come from external history, since the biblical historians have subordinated his story to that of David. They allot only a small amount of narrative to him [1 Kgs 3-11].

SOLOMON AND NARRATIVE SPIRITUALITY

Within these nine chapters it is possible to identify many stories and traditions which derive from tenth or ninth century BCE scribes. They would have supported Solomon and his monarchy, so their optimistic view of him might rival the tone set by the authors of the story of David's rise. This court history begins quite optimistically.

> *1 Kings*
> [2:46b] So the kingdom was established in the hand of Solomon.
> [3:1] Solomon made a marriage alliance with Pharaoh king of Egypt; he took Pharaoh's daughter, and brought her into the city of David, until he had finished building his own house and the house of the LORD and the wall around Jerusalem.
> [3:2] The people were sacrificing at the high places . . .

The summary note in 1 Kgs 2:46b ends a complicated narration of events leading toward Solomon's coronation as king [1 Kgs 1-2]. Now we hear about his marriage patterns. By taking a daughter of Pharaoh as his wife, Solomon displayed great political wisdom, securing political alliances through royal marriage.

Solomon at Gibeon [1 Kgs 3:1-15]

The entire Solomonic section really takes its cue from the next story. Solomon's dream-vision at Gibeon associates him with the worship at the sanctuary and also assures him of God's gift of wisdom [1 Kgs 3:2-15]. A very early story recounts Solomon's night dream after he had offered magnificent sacrifices. In this vision God invites him to "ask what I shall give you" [1 Kgs 3:5], to which he replies: "give thy servant then a *discerning heart* (translation mine) to govern thy people, that I may discern between good and evil; for who is able to govern this thy great people?" [1 Kgs 3:9] Solomon's simple request so delights God that he receives not only wisdom but also riches and honor, benefits a king would be expected to seek. Then Solomon awakens, realizing it had been a dream [1 Kgs 3:15a]. This charming story reminds its hearers of the revelatory power of dream visions, of the insignificance of power and wealth, of the divine origin of Solomon's gift, and of the importance of wisdom for able governance. All of these factors reinforce the optimistic view of Solomon's reign.

Solomon's Judgment [1 Kgs 3:16-28]

The wisdom which Solomon had sought and received at Gibeon manifests itself in the next story. Two harlots come before the king, seeking a judgment from him. This famous story pivots around a grotesque dispute between two women concerning two infants, one dead and one living. Each claims the live infant which they brought into the court as her own. Both argue that the dead infant is the other's. Each tells a story in which she holds the other woman responsible for the death of her infant. On the basis of these charges and stories the king is expected to determine who was the genuine mother of the living child.

In this story, Solomon displays the marvelous gifts he had sought. His lack of arrogance emerges in his personal concern for these two women. He has received a discerning heart which appears in his ability to listen well to them; notice how accurately he repeats their stories. But the heart of the story comes in v. 26: "Then the woman whose son was alive said to the king, because her *maternal compassion burned for her son* (translation mine) . . . 'Give her the living child and by no means slay it.' " This king displays a God-given capacity to reach decisions for the benefit of his people.

Solomon's wisdom consists in recognizing that the woman who showed compassion was the mother. This Hebrew word for "compassion," *rachamim*, is closely related to the word for "womb," *rechem*. The storyteller suggests that Solomon was able to recognize one woman's compassion as maternal, for it came from the womb. Solomon's accuracy thus hinges on his ability to make distinctions based on his observations of these women. The real mother, Solomon knows, values the infant's life above her own relation to the child. This king exhibits an awareness of compassion. This was the quality which his father David had lacked when dealing with Tamar's rape or Uriah's loss. Solomon's wisdom first showed itself in his ability to discern the mother by observing the maternal relationship. His prayer at Gibeon has clearly been answered by God. In his first action as king the life of the infant which he preserved stands as symbol of this king's gift and contribution to Israel. He has embodied a leadership style which bases decisions on genuine respect for human life.

Solomon's judgment uncannily provides us with another source for our spiritual journeys—the wisdom of women. In the story of the two harlots the wisdom of women can be intuited from the story. Solomon's real achievement lies in his recognition of maternal wisdom: a genuine mother values the life of the child more than her relationship with that child. Part of Solomon's genius lies in his bringing to discernment his comprehension of the women's experience. He focused on the relational values which he intuited from the women's stories. This story of his judgment in court subordinates the rules of logic, interrogation, and evidence to the experience and spirituality of women.

Solomon's Administration [1 Kgs 4:1-28]

The narration now turns from Solomon's portrait to the monarchy which he headed. The description of his administration contains long lists of officials who supported the structure of the kingdom [1 Kgs 4:1-28]. This tremendous growth in power and prestige must seem a very positive accomplishment, except for an ominous note about forced labor [1 Kgs 4:6]. Solomon's bureaucracy did not benefit all Israel, but the storyteller only provides hints about the social stratification which began at this time. Courtly enthusiasm apparently downplays the negative effects of Solomon's social and economic changes.

An author's point of view also manifests itself in the order of the events which are described. So we can also learn how the early tradition viewed Solomon's accomplishments by considering the placement of these lists in 1 Kings 4. This is the second story about Solomon, after his dream at Gibeon, which embodies the gift he had sought there: "a discerning heart to govern thy people" [1 Kgs 3:9]. Solomon's administrative abilities appear to these scribes as God's answer to his prayer.

Solomon's Wisdom [1 Kgs 4:29-34]

Jewish tradition has long associated Solomon with the gift

of wisdom and reflection. It has linked him to three important books of the Old Testament: Song of Songs, Ecclesiastes, and Proverbs. In the Greek Bible a fourth book, the Wisdom of Solomon, continues this view of him. In various ways these connections of Solomon and wisdom find a source in the next few verses of the court story of Solomon.

1 Kings 4
[29] And God gave Solomon wisdom and understanding beyond measure, and largeness of mind like the sand on the seashore, [30] so that Solomon's wisdom surpassed the wisdom of all the people of the east, and all the wisdom of Egypt.

The text continues with a listing of evidence of his wisdom: he had composed numerous proverbs, songs, psalms, riddles, as well as natural wisdom, knowledge of the entire universe and its creatures. All of this comes from God, who had answered Solomon's request.

This section praises God as source of Solomon's wisdom. In the early days of the monarchy court theologians readily associated literary success and teaching ability with divine favor. These qualities also form part of the explanation of his success as a ruler. Here God's gift to Solomon assured his success as ruler and provided his monarchy with optimism and security. Finally, his fame would spread throughout the world, so that people would come "from all peoples to hear the wisdom of Solomon, and from all the kings of the earth, who had heard of his wisdom" [4:34].

Solomon and Sheba [1 Kgs 10:1-25]

The rich praise of Solomon's wisdom prepares us well for the famous story of the Queen of Sheba's visit to Solomon [10:1-25]. Her visit prolongs the optimistic picture of Solomon's reign, demonstrating how he "excelled all the kings of the earth in riches and in wisdom" [1 Kgs 10:23]. This story emerges from Solomon's followers, the same court scribes who highly valued judicial and organizational wisdom. Solomon's combination of wealth and wisdom reminds us of his nocturnal revelation at Gibeon and his use of that wisdom to save the life of the harlot's child; Solomon's positive assessment by these wisdom scribes is funded by the same qualities observed in earlier stories. We see this in the praise offered by the Queen of Sheba: "Because the LORD loved Israel forever, he has made you king, that you may exercise justice and righteousness" [1 Kgs 10:9b]. Unlike David, the final verdict of Israel's courtly tradition on Solomon seems wholeheartedly positive.

The early Solomonic story provides us with another vivid resource for narrative spirituality of the monarchy. It points to important sources of revelation. Solomon's dream at Gibeon offers an example of his experience of God in a dream; it may suggest for us the revelatory possibilities of dreams. The same story points also to crucial spiritual desires. Solomon asks for the gift of wisdom for the benefit of others; he begs for it before all other gifts—certainly before prestige, power, and possessions. His petition challenges us to beg for the gifts most appropriate to our life settings. His experience of God's graciousness gives us hope when we seek humbly in prayer. These stories portray Solomon as a hero of the spiritual life and they invite us to imitate his humility and his acceptance of divine graciousness. This portrait of Solomon provides hope for today as it did for his generation.

Solomon's wisdom calls us to reflect on the presence of such gifts in contemporary leaders of society, of governments, of churches. Administrative wisdom may be sought out as a gift from God. Great accomplishments are those which benefit the people more than the leader. Discernment in the pursuit of justice also becomes a matter of spiritual as well as intellectual maturity. Wisdom in other areas of life, especially in physical, natural, and social sciences, provides another sign of God's gift to a leader. The Solomonic portrait refutes any stereotype of the religious pietist as the most graced person.

The narrator also described peoples and rulers from other lands flocking to Jerusalem to meet Solomon [1 Kgs 4:34]. These stories focus not only on the king's prestige, but also on the joy which his wisdom engendered among other humans. Wisdom and monarchy are here placed together, as if they belonged together. Finally, wisdom may pursue its own goals, but from these stories we learn that they are all gifts of God given not for personal benefit but for the joy and wonder of all.

SOLOMON AND DEUTERONOMIC SPIRITUALITY

The deuteronomic preachers could not remember Solomon with such trust and hope as did the scribes of his own court. They and their ancestors had experienced too much pain and frustration because of the arrogance, pride, and wealth of many kings. The Deuteronomists flourished in the seventh century BCE, after the northern kingdom of Israel had fallen in 722 BCE. In this century the Assyrian empire posed an even greater threat to Judah in the south. In their historical and religious reflections, the Deuteronomists lay much of the blame for Judah's trials on the monarchs themselves.

The court story showed reserve when reporting negative aspects of Solomon's behavior; its remark on forced labor [1 Kgs 4:6] could be taken as gently critical. Deuteronomic writers, by contrast, emphasize the problems created by their monarchs. For example, I suspect that Solomon's political marriage with an Egyptian woman [1 Kgs 3:1] would prove neuralgic in the days of King Josiah. His action reestablished ties through marriage with the land of Israel's ancient servitude and oppression, the land from which the LORD had brought them out. From this abuse and many others like it springs the deuteronomic notion that the king should not "cause the people to return to Egypt" [Deut 17:16b]. Returning to Egypt was not a geographical journey for the Deuteronomists; rather, it implies returning to a set of values and way of life which had once oppressed them. Kings who bound Israel too closely to alien customs were rightly suspect in Israel. Subjects and advisors of the monarch who approved such relations also evoked the ire of these preachers.

The "High Place" at Gibeon [1 Kgs 3:2-15]

Sacrificing at the high places presents another problem for the Deuteronomists. The deuteronomic law (Deut 12-26) begins with the command to centralize worship in Jerusalem.

Deuteronomy 12

[2] You shall surely destroy all the places where the nations whom you shall dispossess served their gods, upon the high mountains and upon the hills and under every green tree; [3] you shall tear down their altars and dash in pieces their pillars, and burn their Asherim with fire; you shall hew down the graven images of their gods, and destroy their name out of that place . . . [5] But you shall seek the place which the LORD your God will choose out of all your tribes to put his name and make his habitation there; [6] thither you shall go . . . .

Although many high places in Judah provided local sites for worship of the LORD, the demand for a single place of worship raised questions about the "high places." They served as reminders of Canaanite worship, so they had to be extirpated. The deuteronomic historian accuses many of Judah's kings with failing to take away the high places: Rehoboam, Asa, Jehoshaphat, Jehoash, Amaziah, Azariah, Jotham, and Manasseh.

Since Gibeon was described as "the great high place" [1 Kgs 3:4], the Solomon story could raise doubts for people of the generation of the Deuteronomists. If Solomon worshiped at high places like Gibeon, why was it forbidden for them? Historians would remember that Gibeon had been a central shrine for the tribes before the monarchy existed. They could have given an erudite explanation. They could simply point out that Solomon could not have done otherwise until the temple was constructed. But they display even more caution. At the story's conclusion we hear an orthodox version of Solomon's cultic activity. When Solomon came to Jerusalem "he stood before the ark of the covenant of the LORD" [1 Kgs 3:15]. They bring him into line with the practice and spirituality of their day.

These tensions in the biblical text demonstrate a problem which many people have faced. Why is our life more constrained and regulated than those of our forebears in faith? The preacher seems to answer: you have been given more than your ancestors, so more shall be required of you. Another important spiritual issue arises here—comparing the spirituality of one generation with that of another. Two solutions are applied here. These preachers touch up Solomon's portrait, showing his reverence for the ark. But they dare not change the story completely, for the old site retained deep spiritual meaning: there Solomon met God, and that manifestation shines forth. Even as they exhort a new spiritual vision, they retain an older one.

In the Gibeon story the Deuteronomists clarify the view of Solomon in other ways. Enthusiastic hope for this ruler now rests not only on his wisdom but on his love of God. Solomon begins to resemble his father David, especially his relationship with God. The Deuteronomists make some important additions to the court version of Solomon's prayer at Gibeon. In the prayer below I have italicized typical deuteronomic language in order to demonstrate the homiletic and theological tendencies in it.

> *1 Kings 3*
>
> [6] And Solomon said, 'Thou hast shown great and steadfast love to *thy servant David my father*, because *he walked before thee in faithfulness, in righteousness, and in uprightness of heart* toward thee; and thou hast kept for him this great and steadfast love, and hast given him a son to sit on his throne *this day*. [7] And now O LORD my God, thou hast made thy servant king in place of David my father, although I am but a little child; I do not know how to go out or come in. [8] And thy servant is in the midst of thy people whom thou hast *chosen*, a great people, that cannot be numbered or counted for multitude.'

The same writers who make Solomon's prayer more flowery and rhetorical also add two key phrases elsewhere. To begin the story we hear that "Solomon *loved the LORD, walking in the statutes of David his father*" [1 Kgs 3:3]. They conclude it with a stereotypical word of God to the king: "If you will *walk in my ways, keeping my statutes and my commandments, as your father David walked, then I will lengthen your days*" [1 Kgs 3:14].

The effect of their additions is significant. Instead of focusing on Solomon's wisdom, they serve to align him with David, God's servant and the hero of their history. They portray him in the shadow of the promise made explicit to David in the Nathan oracle [2 Sam 7]. The formulas about statutes and commandments shift the royal responsibility from careful discernment to humble obedience to Torah. Torah and covenant have subtly displaced the divine gift of wisdom. Finally, they make the success of Solomon's leadership depend on his abiding by the conditions of the covenant: "if you will walk in My ways". It almost seems that the great leader of the tenth century must be redrawn during the reforms of the seventh century.

How can later generations glory in his multiple marriages, his bureaucracy, his reliance on dreams, his tolerance of other gods in Jerusalem? They know of the monarchy's progressive deterioration after Solomon's time, so how can they imitate his early supporters? They could hardly praise his wisdom so highly when they realize how short-lived was its influence. These preachers realize the folly of people glorying in Solomon's wisdom without searching for it and adhering to it afterwards. The deteriorating situation calls forth a different response—one which they crystalize as covenant faith.

A Second Vision at Gibeon [1 Kgs 9:1-9]

After the construction and dedication of the temple [1 Kgs 6-8; 1 Kgs 9:1-9] the Deuteronomists describe another vision of God by Solomon. God tells him that his prayer has been heard and the temple has been consecrated. But the continuation of his royal line will depend on his fidelity to the covenant.

> *1 Kings 9*
> [4] And as for you, if you will walk before me, as David your father walked, with integrity of heart and uprightness . . . [5] then I will establish your royal throne over Israel for ever, as I promised David your father, saying, 'There shall not fail you a man upon the throne of Israel.' [6] But if you turn aside from following me, you or your children . . . [7] then I will cut off Israel from the land which I have given them; and the house which I have consecrated for my name I will cast out of my sight . . .

For God to place conditions on the royal relationship with God might seem reasonable. One receives in accord with one's acts.

God's promise to David, however, contained no conditional clauses. The king's relationship with God seemed so secure. That promise was spelled out in Nathan's famous oracle to David.

> *2 Samuel 7*
> [12] When your days are fulfilled and you lie down with your fathers, I will raise up your son after you, who shall come forth from your body, and I will establish his kingdom. [13] He shall build a house for my name, and I will establish the throne of his kingdom *forever*. [14] I will be his father, and he shall be my son. When he commits iniquity, I will chasten

> him with the rod ... [15] but I will not take my steadfast
> love from him, as I took it from Saul, whom I put away from
> before you. (emphasis mine)

This divine promise served like a charter for the kings of the
line of David; they should reign forever. If they commit sin,
God would chastise them, but not sever the covenant
relationship of "steadfast love." Hope still remains for the
monarchy.

In view of the covenant with David, God's speech to
Solomon bodes ill for the future. In this second description of
the relation between God and king a decided shift in
language has taken place. The LORD's voice to Solomon
uses language of a conditional covenant: if ... then. Gone is
the sure promise to David and the everlasting relationship,
replaced by a warning to remain obedient. This shift in view
results from centuries of reflection on the monarchy. The
Deuteronomists remember the disintegration of Solomon's
reign, realize its cause in the abrogation of the covenant, and
implicitly exhort their own generation to live their lives
differently. Perhaps these preachers still believe God's promise
to David, but for their day they emphasize the necessity of
royal obedience to God's covenant. In the seventh century
the deuteronomic challenge to demand faithful leadership
replaces an earlier promise of continual divine assistance.
Different social, political, and religious factors called for a
new spiritual emphasis.

Solomon's Wives [1 Kings 11]

The final chapter of the Solomon story provides a
dramatic and chilling conclusion to this royal life. Solomon's

wives came from countries which did not worship the
LORD [1 Kgs 11:1-3], so they become the object of divine
wrath and judgment. His constant catering to them and their
needs lead him away from the focused devotion which the
LORD expects of him [1 Kgs 11:4-8]. The story presents the
problem straightforwardly as a problem of religious orthodoxy
that emerged in Solomon's harem. The divine judgment of
Solomon is unequivocally stated: "the LORD was angry
with Solomon, because his heart had turned away from the
LORD" [1 Kgs 11:9]. The concrete results were devastating.
God raises up political adversaries to Solomon, enemies from
without who wreak havoc on his people [1 Kgs 11:14-25].
Jeroboam's revolt from within [11:26-40] also is a result of
this infidelity.

The expansion of Solomon's harem implicitly poses
another difficulty. In addition to the political alliances which
Solomon had effected through his marriages, the institution
of the royal harem presents social problems. The Deuteronomists know it involved a huge expense, which necessitated
taxes that became heavy and burdensome for the people.
Most of the harem staff, including many of the king's wives
and concubines, came from the less influential and powerful
people of Israel. Their status would resemble that of slaves.
The abuses caused by a royal harem help to explain the
deuteronomic injunction in the "Law of the King": he
should not "multiply wives" for himself [Deut 17:17]. Social
inequity and religious apostasy in Solomon's harem combine,
demonstrating the relationship of religious and social-political
issues. Deuteronomic piety always involves a social vision as
well.

Public life again relates to the king's private life. The effect on Solomon was as devastating as it was for his father David. At the beginning of Solomon's reign the story focused on a personal dream experience of the king, which led to public manifestations of his gifts for leadership. At the end of the Solomon cycle, the storyteller turns to another semi-personal matter, Solomon's harem. It implies that his personal life cannot remain private, much as he might so desire. In the narrator's view, Solomon's marriages lead to corruption of his worship of the LORD.

These marriages signify much more than private matters. They clearly stand at the root of the evil of the Judean monarchy, for Solomon has in some sense inherited the evil tendency of his father David. David's taking of Bathsheba ultimately led to internal division, rebellion, and the gradual destruction of his family. In similar fashion Solomon's marriages with foreign women result in his apostasy and the eventual loss of part of his kingdom from his son [1 Kgs 11:11-12]. Solomon transforms David's weakness with women into a pattern of turning away from the LORD. This homilizing points to the breakdown of marital fidelity and familial trust as key elements in the private and public falling away from integral worship. In their opinion political intrigue and religious deviation seemed constant companions.

The Solomonic narratives, we have discovered, yield no single, monolithic message. As I distinguished an early story set in wisdom circles from later history in homiletic style, some issues for spiritual discernment stand out. All of these derive from new viewpoints produced by reflecting on fresh meaning from the ancient tradition and story.

The Deuteronomists suffered embarrassment over Solomon's worship at the high place at Gibeon. They remind us of the subtle shifts in our religious symbols, especially places of worship. What serves one generation or group well brings trouble to another. They also point to tensions between generations, which can result either from changes that occur too rapidly or from those who resist development. They insisted on one place for the LORD's worship, aiming at the worship of the one God who alone could reconcile their tensions and unite their differences. These preachers invite us to unite together in one LORD today.

In the older stories the spiritual nourishment comes from human experience, considered as a source of God's word. Story and wisdom speak a subtle language, so some people might miss their truths and forget their strictures. Later generations might relax and rely on the wisdom of their forebears, hoping that ancestral truth will suffice for them. The Deuteronomists recognize this human weakness and seek to correct it by renewed focus on the covenant and Torah. They teach us that wisdom is a gift of God to be sought diligently and used graciously in each generation.

The Deuteronomists viewed Solomon's marital life as crucial to his life and leadership. Centuries of ineffective rule by kings taught them the problems of Solomon's ways with women. The politics involved in his marital alliances continue to plague rulers and leaders, and they impact the lives of those whom they serve. The social and economic problems caused by the royal harem have their counterparts in our day. Women still experience different rights and prerogatives than men in the marriage laws of many countries. Israel's experience of idolatry because of the royal harem reminds us of the delicate and necessary role of spirituality and faith in healthy marriages. Solomon poses challenges for us.

Finally, Solomon's life demonstrates the difficulty of treating private life as separate from one's work and public affairs. This is not to say that everthing we do or say ought to be made public, but the quality of our private lives does affect our families and communities and particularly any role of ministry or leadership.

The Chronicler's Spirituality of the Monarchy

The Chronicler's spirituality invites us into the world of Judaism. After the experience of the Babylonian exile and the return to Judah under Cyrus the Persian, the small Jewish community felt new tensions and struggles. Their need for spiritual nourishment led them to reincorporate the teachings of their deuteronomic ancestors, just as they had reformulated the early story from court circles. Since they had no king in their day, we might expect them to view the monarchy more theoretically and nostalgically than their deuteronomic forebears.

The Chronicler had the books of Samuel and Kings as sources for his interpretation. We should inquire how he represented the ancient sources for his post-exilic generation. Like any good preacher, the Chronicler picks and chooses from among stories and lists of temple and court personnel. The specific choices made for this history indicate what seemed important to the writer.

There are different ways to use biblical materials in a homiletic presentation, including presenting the same stories in a different chronological order, adding new details or sections, and omitting parts of the original text. Any substantial change in the sacred story signifies an area of emphasis by the writer. I assume that the Chronicler made such changes in order to address the particular spiritual, religious, and social problems of his age. We will examine the Chronicler's spirituality especially by observing the order of events he created when he rewrote the Davidic history.

I choose to focus my comments on one monarch whose stories we have already studied: David. Since we have already asked about the spiritual focus of the early court narratives, and then about emphases of the deuteronomic historians, we can move to the Chronicler's post-exilic concerns. The Chronicler arranged the David traditions with a new order of events, and his changes will lead an audience to view David's monarchy differently. Other changes in the earlier history will also prove useful.

DAVID IN THE BOOKS OF CHRONICLES

The David Story, beginning with 1 Chronicles 10, is really the first narrative in Chronicles. The preceding material in 1 Chronicles 1-9 consists of genealogical lists. This historian relates Israel's early history up to the time of David through lists which resemble family trees. As a result, the Chronicler views all of Israel's history—even the whole universe—as building up to David's story [1 Chr 10-29]. David's story, then, has become the central truth for this Jewish community.

How do we evaluate and integrate this tendency to make David so central? Biblical scholar Walter Brueggemann suggests an example from contemporary psychoanalytic experience.[6] For the sake of isolating issues and making progress, those who are in therapy often consider their own reality as the center or core of "their universe." Ultimately they recognize that their selective perception of reality allows them to focus constructively on their world, perhaps to reconstruct it, and then to relate more widely with their community and environment. Perhaps the Chronicler's focus on David provided for fifth-century Jews just such a clarifying focus. We could judge the Chronicler's effort a bit more positively if we attended to its therapeutic intent. If we could learn what features of the David story nurtured the people for whom the Chronicler wrote we might find nourishment in them for our spiritual journeys.

The Chronicler begins the David story at 2 Samuel 5:1-11, when "all the elders of Israel" met David at Hebron. They entered into covenant with him and "anointed David king over Israel, according to the word of the LORD by Samuel" [1 Chr 11:3]. Recall that 1-2 Samuel showed more interest in the stories of David's youth, his tensions with Saul, and his growing strength in the southern Judean desert. The Chronicler, by contrast, shows no concern about the social and political process that led Israel to yearn for a king. First Chronicles does not describe the liberating freshness of David's rise to power, nor his gradual acceptance by all the tribes of Israel. Instead this version explains what it means for all the universe to "wait for" David.

---

[6]Brueggemann, *David's Truth*, p. 100. As an historical example he mentions the tendency of some in Reformation churches to imagine that church history began with Martin Luther.

Here David lacks both the opposition of Saul and the encouragement of people like Abigail. Like the figures carved on portals of the twelfth-century cathedral at Chartres, this David stands as an object of contemplation rather than as model for everyday life. Lacking the discrete historical context or the supporting actors of Samuel and Kings, this David seems at ease in the worship setting. There the post-exilic community found itself most free to express its Jewish identity and aspirations. Chronicles, then, invites Jews to bring David to worship, to the liturgical assembly, and there to feed their hopes in a fashion least likely to cause trouble with the Persians who ruled Palestine when the Chronicler was writing. For Jews of the fifth and fourth centuries BCE, worship constituted the best possible form of public expression.

David's Coronation [1 Chronicles 11-12]

The Chronicler elaborates on David's coronation in 1 Chronicles 11-12. There he combines lists of the warriors who followed David with two stories contained in 2 Samuel. David concluded the coronation with a three-day feast in Hebron for all Israel, a time of great "eating and drinking," "for there was joy in Israel" [1 Chr 12:40]. All the details combine to paint a picture of David's immediate designation by the LORD and acceptance by all the people: this king truly embodies the divine will for Israel. The Chronicler seems less intent on describing ancient history than on offering hope to post-exilic Jews. The saving portrait of David provides that model for the Chronicler's audience.

David's Solidarity *[1 Chr 11:15-19]*

Since the Chronicler paid no attention to stories about David's rise to power, it is surprising to find him telling the story of the three chiefs who bring water for David to drink [1 Chr 11:15-19; parallel in 2 Sam 23:13-17]. They had responded to David's wish that "someone would give me water to drink from the well of Bethlehem" [1 Chr 11:17]. Bravely they breached the Philistine lines to fulfill his wish. When they approach David with this precious water he pours it onto the ground [1 Chr 11:18]. The historian gives us the king's words.

> *1 Chronicles 11*
> [19] "Far be it from me before my God that I should do this. Shall I drink the lifeblood of these men? For at the risk of their lives they brought it." Therefore he would not drink it.

Did David's gesture signify rejection of their effort? Rather, his explanation points to a profound realization, that his men obtained this water at great risk to their lives. Consequently he would not devalue their courage by simply slaking his thirst.

David's intuition about the cost of this water leads him to decline enjoyment of that which his men could not enjoy. Here David rejects a chance to set himself over his men. His solidarity with them increases because of this action and renders him more attractive to them and more authoritative in the eyes of all. For the Chronicler this story not only provides motivation for those who support his cause, it also demonstrates another effect of the LORD's choice of this man as king.

David Leads Worship [1 Chronicles 13-15]

The narratives in 2 Samuel 5-6 provide essential insights into the growth of the Davidic monarchy over all Israel, and the Chronicler grasps their importance. First Chronicles presents these chapters as the initial stage of David's reign, but the order in which they appear specifies important homiletic concerns of the historian. In 2 Samuel 5, David increases his harem and adds to his military victories over the Philistines; in the next chapter he prepares to retrieve the Ark from Kiriath-jearim [2 Sam 6:2-11]. The Chronicler puts worship before all else by reversing the order of events. 1 Chronicles 13 describes David's preparation to move the ark, followed by notice of David's marriages (without mention of concubines!) and military accomplishments in 1 Chronicles 14. Worship forms David's first concern in Chronicles, perhaps not from an historical sense but because of religious needs of fifth-century Jews. The Chronicler portrays David as a leader who understands the spiritual needs of his people and acts to meet them.

The folksy, dancing parade of David and the ark of 2 Samuel 6:12-19 has become an elaborate liturgical procession in 1 Chronicles 15:1-16:43. Since I will discuss these passages in Chapter Four, only one incident interests us here: Michal's anger at David when she saw him dancing before the ark [1 Chr 15:29].The Samuel narrative went on to explain her reaction, for she accused him of honoring "himself today, uncovering himself today before the eyes of his servants' maids, as one of the vulgar fellows shamelessly uncovers himself" [2 Sam 6:20]. But the David of Chronicles can hardly be accused of public indecency: he was wearing a "robe of fine linen, as also were the Levites . . . and David wore a linen ephod" [1 Chr 15:27]. If this is how David appeared, the reader of Chronicles wonders why Michal, his wife "despised him in her heart" [1 Chr 15:29].

Earlier generations during the monarchy probably over-looked David's exuberant resemblance to dancing in honor of Baal, though his wife Michal had not. Later, in the days of liturgy and processions, her attitude seemed petulant since his concern for worship of the LORD had been regularized. Few could find fault with this leader of worship. He had distributed food to his co-celebrants [1 Chr 16:2-3] and directed the Levites to chant psalms of thanksgiving for God's great gifts to all Israel [1 Chr 16:7-36]. By dismissing the reasons for Michal's anger, the Chronicler portrays David in a far better light and Michal in a poorer light. As we will notice elsewhere, the Chronicler often whitewashed David in order to enhance his stature for later Jewish congregations.

God as Israel's King [1 Chronicles 17]

In Nathan's oracle to David [2 Sam 7:1-17; 1 Chr 17:1-15] attentive listeners will discern another very important change. Near its end, David hears: "your house and your kingdom shall be made sure for ever before me" [2 Sam 7:16]; but a later generation heard "but I will confirm him in my house and in my kingdom for ever" [1 Chr 17:14]. Israel's real king is God, not David or Solomon or their posterity. Monarchy in the Chronicler's Israel cannot be subjected to questioning: it comes from the LORD, and its return after Exile is assured. For post-exilic Jews the surety of God's care for David's dynasty provided motivation for their work of reconstructing Jewish society.

After the Nathan oracle, the two histories diverge widely. Second Samuel 8 and 10 provide summaries of David's amazing military accomplishments. Second Samuel 9, however, presents David as he showed "loyalty" to his friend Jonathan's son, Mephibosheth. After this follows the very human portrait of David in 2 Samuel 11-20 and 1 Kings 1-2. Chronicles parades David's military prowess before his audience, combining various older reports in 1 Chronicles 18-20. But the example of David's loyalty was omitted, as was the rest of 2 Samuel 9-20 with its emphasis on the personal and familial life of David.

What a different David was preached to this generation! What had happened to the story of a king experienced in lust and adultery, given to weakness when the behavior of his children demanded firmness? Chronicles transforms him into a military hero whose exploits gradually provided a settled situation in which Israel could focus its attention on worship and a temple. David's final accomplishments in 1 Chronicles all concern worship [1 Chr 22-29]. Perhaps the Chronicler was too much a preacher to include a brutally honest picture of David's flaws and familial breakdown. Another explanation also presents itself. The later chapters of 2 Samuel do not mention worship or contain explicit theological statements. The secular events of David's court and family life do not buttress the liturgical face of David, so this omission of David's weakness fits nicely with the Chronicler's interest in worship.

How can we appropriate the Chronicler's vision of David's role as monarch? Do we simply assert that his commitment to public liturgy replaced the royal role when it was no longer possible during the Persian rule? We might, on the other hand, conclude that David's authentic reign included a liturgical dimension. Then, genuine rule would be rooted in worship of the LORD. Here David's reign speaks both to our own exercise of leadership and ministry, and also to the hopes which provide us with energy. For those who do not exercise a ministry of leadership, their service may find its analog in the service and ministry of the Levites, whom the Chronicler carefully lists [e.g. 1 Chr 23, 25, 26]. They cared for the sacred symbols of divine presence and led the singing, music, and dance at Israel's temple. Their role in Israel's communal worship symbolizes the significance of sacristans, musicians, lectors and many others today whose care fosters liturgical prayer. The Chronicler's portrayal of David actually includes and inspires many more members of society than most readers might expect.

The portrait of David in Chronicles also speaks comfortingly to those whose lives and rights are greatly curtailed by alien authorities. A community of prayer offers meaning and identity when political organization has collapsed. David's sign of solidarity with the men who risked their lives to bring him water provides a real test of one's readiness for leadership. The call to lead, to minister can best be discerned in those who are willing to serve, to stand alongside their sisters and brothers. The Chronicler's surprising inclusion of this story shows concern for solidarity as a basic spiritual stance, especially in times of alienation and loss of power for self-determination.

The Chronicler's spirituality also draws nourishment from Nathan's oracle, that God will establish David in God's house, not the earthly king's, as in 2 Samuel 7. This profound realization that the LORD reigns as Israel's real king invites audiences of this book in all ages to reflect on the final source of social and political authority. It is the LORD alone. That message bears repeating even today.

Conclusion

After pondering this remarkable variety of traditions about the roles of Israel's kings, we return to the homiletic spirituality of the monarchy. How did the Deuteronomists and the Chronicler appreciate the monarchy as a source of faithful response to God? For each of these groups the personal, enthusiastic experience of monarchy under David and Solomon was little more than a memory. As the centuries passed, the glories of Solomon's reign faded. Wisdom in governance, discernment, and protection of the rights of Israelites had led to high praise in earlier days. Later teachers of Israel, however, realized that they could not offer a complete experience of God's *shalom* for this people. In the many marriages of Solomon they recognized the seeds of the monarchy's later demise, due to royal infidelity to the LORD. As the Deuteronomists told Solomon's story, they emphasized the conditions on which blessings depended. As they retold his story they realized that the everlasting promise to David was too good to be true. Even David's covenant depended on the king's adherence to Torah, the statutes given to David. The Deuteronomists challenge us to discern whether the astute, articulate, clever leader also possesses a humble devotion to the religious and spiritual roots of their people. If Torah piety is demanded of kings, how much more for the rest of us?

The Chronicler's penchant for pinning hopes on a deceased leader might strike us as a bit odd. Particularly strange is a monarch whose major interest seems to be liturgical! But for a generation which had no king, this preacher invited the assembly to remember a time when the ruling powers affirmed their worship of the LORD, instead of attempting ever so subtly to thwart it. How should they remember such times? By constant and faithful attention to the riches of liturgical prayer and by trusting that communal worship would bring forgiveness to those in need of it. The Chronicler, finally, discovered in David genuine nourishment for a community which lacked pride and hope. The Chronicler also viewed David as trusting in the divine promise, and as living in humble and practical solidarity with others. Today, when many people experience similar alienation, these values of monarchic spirituality stand as gifts offered for our own lives.

Part II

The Temple

The story of the Jerusalem Temple begins with the monarchy in the tenth century BCE. As a descriptive term, temple refers to three different structures, all constructed on the same site, known today as the Temple Mount. Since 70 CE, when Herod's temple was destroyed by the Romans during the Jewish revolt, no Jewish temple has stood at that location. Since that time, however, this mount has supported a Roman temple, a Christian basilica, and a Moslem mosque. To this day the location remains sacred to the three major religious groups of the area—Jews, Christians, and Moslems.

Although the physical structure has ceased to exist, the Temple has remained a vibrant memory and a profound spiritual motif for both Jews and Christians. Our interest in this study, however, draws us back to the books of Samuel and Kings. There we will search for the Temple's spiritual significance in the historical books of the Old Testament. This brief introduction will allow us to review quickly the history of the Jerusalem temple and the various literary witnesses to the Temple in the Old Testament.

The books of Kings [1 Kgs 5-8] and Chronicles [2 Chr 2-7] describe the edifice constructed in Jerusalem by King Solomon, probably between 957-950 BCE. It stood for the duration of Israel's monarchy, until the destruction of Jerusalem and the temple during the second Babylonian invasion of 587-586 BCE. With the loss of the first temple, Israel's people—both in the Exile and in Judah—lacked a worship center which could bind them together.

During the Exile, Ezekiel's profound vision of the restored Jerusalem opened one avenue of hope for his destitute people. His vision of the renewed Jerusalem [Ezekiel 40-48] centers around a reconstructed Temple. In the new Jerusalem everything should center around the Temple. The holiness he accorded the Temple seems natural for a writer of a priestly family.

After the Exile, Zerubbabel constructed a second temple. Although its modest dimensions disappointed most elderly Jews who recalled Solomon's temple, its religious significance grew, especially among priestly and Levitical groups. Through the various political upheavals which shook Judah, the Temple remained. In 168 BCE the Seleucid ruler Antiochus Epiphanes desecrated the Temple by introducing pagan worship. Frustration over this sacrilege combined with nationalistic passion to fuel the Maccabean revolt. At its successful conclusion the Temple was restored for Jewish worship.

As part of his extensive building program, Herod the Great rebuilt the Jerusalem Temple around 20 CE. In effect, this was the third temple. He decorated it lavishly, seeking to restore the temple to its ancient splendor. This edifice was the one which Titus' army destroyed when it captured and sacked Jerusalem in 70 CE. Although Jewish groups attempted to rebuild the temple in 132-135 CE (the second Jewish revolt), in 362-363 CE (during the reign of Julian the

Apostate), and in the seventh century CE, none succeeded. Herod's third temple stood as the last temple.

The religious and spiritual significance of the Temple pushes our inquiry beyond the history of the edifice. We learn about the temple primarily from biblical texts, many of which aim less at narrating its story than describing the ritual life of the temple. Concern for the temple and its worship runs high in a number of traditions: the priestly tradition in the Pentateuch, Ezekiel, the Psalms, Deuteronomy, Kings, and Chronicles. Some of those traditions emphasize different religious meanings than did the authors of Kings and Chronicles, which are our focus here. Their message can help us discern the meaning of the temple in the histories.

Israel's priestly writers gifted us with the priestly history, the version of the Pentateuch which we read today. In the books of Genesis, Exodus, Numbers, and Leviticus their view of Israel's early days owes much to their experience of the temple. They viewed their life even in the desert period (before entering the land) through the prism of worship in the temple. Exodus 25-31 contains precise and elaborate instructions for the tabernacle in the wilderness, and the work was completed in Exodus 35-40. The priestly attention to the dimensions of the tabernacle and ark reminds us of the temple in which they ministered. Their description of cultic objects and rituals suggests a later writer finding traces of the worship he knew in ancient days. Although modern scholars have largely neglected the priestly tradition, recent studies have built on insights from anthropological studies. Some researchers take this tradition more seriously, particularly the holiness system focused on the temple and the priesthood.

The book of Psalms provides rich resources for our

knowledge of the temple. Some have referred to the Psalter as a hymnal for the second temple (i.e. after the return from Exile). Whether or not these psalms should be considered so late, we may agree that the Psalms witness to the spiritual motifs and the religious rituals of the Jerusalem temple. In the following passages I have indicated important motifs in italic print.

> I was glad when they said to me, "Let us go to the *house of the Lord*" [Ps 122:1].
> How lovely is *thy dwelling place*, O LORD of hosts! [Ps 84:1].
> I would rather be a doorkeeper in the *house of my God* than dwell in the tents of wickedness [Ps 84:10b].

In these and many other psalms which originated in the worship of the Jerusalem temple we perceive a strong sense of God's abiding/residing presence in this holy house. Since the temple site is often referred to as Mount Zion, many scholars refer to the sense of God's dwelling there as Zion theology.

The house of God on earth, however, is not a peculiarly Israelite notion. Ample evidence exists to show that this feature of the temple (and of Zion theology in the Psalter) comes not only from ancient Israelite sources and traditions, but was shared with Israel's neighbors. There are numerous similarities between the description of this temple—for what we know of the Jerusalem temple comes from literary sources—and the remains and stories of temples of the Canaanite gods Baal and El. The temple in Jerusalem seems to share in the general notion of a two-tiered cosmos; there the earthly temple serves as a mirror or reflection of the god's house in the heavens. From this view one can easily move to the idea that the divinity dwells in the temple. Elements of this pervasive worldview appear in some psalms, especially those classified as hymns of praise.

In the last century, archaeological discoveries have yielded building plans for several Semitic temples. After comparing this evidence with the biblical accounts, many have suggested that the plan of the Jerusalem temple resembles other ancient temples in the region. A mixture of Israelite and Near Eastern concepts of temple make even more sense if—as some historians claim—Solomon constructed a place of worship on the very site of an ancient Canaanite temple.

As with the monarchy, the Hebrew Scriptures do not provide a single, clear notion of the meaning of the temple. We can find aspects of belief in the temple as God's house in the Psalms, and even in the books of Samuel, Kings and Chronicles. But these books will generally teach us differently, pointing to the temple as house of prayer, a place for communion with the LORD.

When we turn to the books of Kings and Chronicles, a sensitive listening can reveal elements of story and preaching about the temple. In these next two chapters I will proceed as before, focusing first on narrative spirituality in stories which seem to originate in early court circles. Court scribes probably were attracted to temple traditions because of the closeness and interaction between temple and palace. For David a temple would represent the fruit of a divine promise to him and his progeny. Solomon, on the other hand, could see it both as the fulfillment of the promise to David and as a manifestation of God's gift of wisdom to him. Chapter Three, accordingly, concerns narratives which offer their view of the Temple project.

The homilizing of the Deuteronomists beckoned Israel to a profound fidelity to the covenant. The deuteronomic preaching in 1 Kings clearly addresses the violations committed by temple personnel who substituted religious rituals in place of prayer to God, whose name dwells there. At the same time it condemns alien practices and rituals—especially temple prostitution—which had infiltrated temple worship. For the generation of Jews which returned from Exile in Babylon, the Chronicler needed to apply a different type of exhortation. Now that the temple stood as the only living symbol of their ancient faith, its meaning had to extend to include ever more of Israel's reality. Chronicles invites Jews of its era to public prayer in the temple as the most concrete way to express hope. In the preaching of these two generations we discover a homiletic spirituality of the temple. Chapter Four will concern the message these preachers offer.

3

THE TEMPLE AND DIVINE PRESENCE: NARRATIVE SPIRITUALITY OF THE JERUSALEM TEMPLE

Governments generally develop symbols of their authority, and Israel proved no exception to this pattern. Once the monarchic style of governance had been established in Israel, the proper symbols had to be erected to house the ruler and honor the divinity responsible for this people and place. Many peoples do this by construction projects in which they demonstrate their core values and hopes through the effort and resources they invest in buildings, both public and religious. For many of Solomon's subjects it would seem only natural to provide the ark of God with a more permanent resting place. As the palace provided the king's residence so did the temple offer a location for the ark, the symbol of God's presence among this people.

We will begin our exploration with the earlier reaction to the idea of building a temple: Nathan's oracle to David [2 Sam 7:1-17]. This encounter with David hints at a questioning attitude toward the idea of housing the ark in a permanent structure. A generation later, however, a fresh group of scribes from Solomon's Jerusalem provided a very detailed and positive remembrance of Solomon's construction of the first temple [1 Kgs 5-8]. In this chapter, then, I will begin with David's desire to construct a suitable location for the LORD and then continue with the elaborate temple story of Solomon's time. A narrative spirituality of the Temple will be the goal of this chapter, so the texts I will present are those which emerged early in the monarchy, long before the times of the Deuteronomists. In these texts from the early days of the monarchy we may expect to find open questions and tensions which paved the way for later preachers to ponder.

David's Concern for Worship

A long description of David's growing strength and ability to lead occupies the narrator of 1 Samuel 16—2 Samuel 1. Next we read of his final rise to leadership of the southern kingdom [2 Sam 2:1-11] and then of all Israel [2 Sam 5:1-16]. After the stealthy capture of Jerusalem, the narrator lists the events of the Israelite entry into the city. Next, David renames the city Zion "city of David" after himself and builds up the city [2 Sam 5:9]. The storyteller comments: "And David became greater and greater, for the LORD, the God of hosts, was with him" [2 Sam 5:10]. Then a series of accomplishments in Jerusalem add to the luster of his monarchy. Hiram of Tyre's messengers bring cedar and construct a palace for David [2 Sam 5:11]. David contracts more marriages [2 Sam 5:13-16] and defeats the Philistine enemies [2 Sam 5:17-25].

Then we hear another interpretive remark: "David perceived that the LORD had established him king over Israel, and that he had exalted his kingdom for the sake of his people Israel" [2 Sam 5:12]. It is not enough that God helped David in all his undertakings; now we learn that God's motive in elevating him was the strengthening of all Israel. Therefore the fate of Israel depends in some way on David.

David's stature further increases when he brings the ark of God into Jerusalem. From its lonely isolation in the house of Obed-edom he leads a procession into the capital city [2 Sam 6:1-15]. Now that his own residence and defenses are established, it is time to focus on the symbols of religion. The ark which Israel had taken into battle provides an aura of antiquity, security, and unity for those who trace their origins back to Egypt and the Exodus experience.

The story offers further incidents for reflection. In 2 Samuel 6:16-23 we hear poignant narratives about the reactions to David's processional with the ark. Michal, David's wife and Saul's daughter, berates his jubilation before the ark as lewd behavior. Eventually, however, she suffers the curse of sterility because of her attitude towards David. Thus this story warns others against cavalier opposition to David's religious practices. After achieving remarkable political success, David suddenly becomes a model of religious behavior. The narrator and the audience of this time do not flinch at the close association of state and religion; they simply understand David's political feats as pretext for similar religious trappings. The early court history of David reveled in his achievements.

David's Plan for a Temple [2 Sam 7:1-17]

The details of David's military and religious entry into Jerusalem set the context for his desire to build God a house. In 2 Samuel 7 we find David in conversation with the prophet Nathan [vv. 1-16]; later the narrator claims to repeat David's prayer after this occasion [vv. 18-29]. David did not face any enemies at this time, external or internal. The story begins simply.

> 2 *Samuel* 7
> [1] Now when the king dwelt in his house, and the LORD had given him rest from all his enemies round about, [2] the king said to Nathan the prophet, "See now, I dwell in a house of cedar, but the ark of God dwells in a tent." [3] And Nathan said to the king, "Go, do all that is in your heart; for the LORD is with you."

After the battles and wars subsided, David and Israel experienced "rest"; a situation of peace allows new questions to be posed.

We assume, of course, that the story refers to David's palace, the house constructed for him by the Tyrian advisers from Hiram. Suddenly David engages in serious discussion with Nathan. The king speaks to the prophet and contrasts his own fine house with the tent of the LORD's ark. Unlike later kings, who often preferred to avoid contact with Israel's prophets, David initiates this conversation. Here is a lucky monarch in Israel, one who consults a religious leader instead of finding himself confronted by one! Civil and religious leaders act together in harmony. The audience of this story also trusts that a positive interplay between these realms can take place.

One wonders what had motivated David's question. Had he just then recognized the incongruity of the situation: his splendid house of cedar, compared to the tent for the ark of God. Cedar is not a wood found in the Judean hills, so it must have been imported from Lebanon through the good graces of Hiram [2 Sam 5:11]. David's extraordinary residence overshadowed the traditional symbol of divine presence in Israel, the tent of meeting. Moreover it identified him with an aura of wealth which was attainable only by the royalty. This story hints at the social and economic stratification already emerging in the monarchic style of existence. Already some signs of the distance between king and people have begun to arise.

In terms appropriate for our day, we may wonder why a powerful government engages in massive projects like churches, monuments, national shrines which take on a peculiarly religious flavor: do they "allow" the masses to share the experience of grandeur which is generally reserved to the elite, to the leaders? Some interpreters view David's desire to build a temple as a political ploy to unite the northern and southern kingdoms. Ultimately they must ask: did he intend to pacify all Israel with a national shrine? Perhaps he intended to offer the general population a share in the grandeur experienced by Israel's elite. Those who see their world from the government's viewpoint tend to explain state projects in such fashion. They might reason, in an ancient "trickle-down" theory, "Whatever helps the government also aids its people."

Gratefully, others in Israel remembered his practical concern for the basic needs of the people. At the celebration with the ark David distributed "a cake of bread, a portion of meat and a cake of raisins" to all the men and women of Israel [2 Sam 6:19]. The story combines a royal concern for sign and symbol with gestures illustrating his attention to the needs of this people. The combination of temple ideology and pragmatic programs paints a very positive portrait.

Other interpreters focus attention on the simple humility displayed by David. They suggest that personal qualities like this one account for much of his greatness. This view of David's interchange with Nathan is also a faithful reading of this text, for David's question apparently impressed the prophet. Nathan said to the king, "Go, do all that is in your heart; for the LORD is with you" [2 Sam 7:3]. As we observed in the Solomon story (Chapter Two) humility before the LORD well befits a monarch in Israel. Descriptive language like this demonstrated David's admirable qualities and edifies the audience of the story. It not only provides them with examples of behavior to imitate, but also builds up their confidence and trust in their government.

Could one listen to David's process of discernment about his building projects and then criticize him for spending too much on national monuments and shrines? The positive tenor of the story makes social criticism very difficult, but it does invite us to reflect on comparable situations. Frequently we are tempted to evaluate leaders on the basis of their stated motives, instead of assessing their achievements or their mistakes. Some officials generate high esteem simply by referring to heroic military service or to personal virtues and values. In either case they appeal to the mood of the populace, to the particular ideology of the present government. It is difficult to criticize openly those who articulate the "state's truth," and David proves no exception in this story. David's "humility" fits nicely into a particular view of government in Israel and spells trouble for those who view the state's responsibilities differently. In the biblical text, such criticisms arise more frequently in the later evaluations of the Deuteronomists and the Chronicler.

All seems well settled: David's reverence toward God invited the positive response of the prophet. But nighttime intervenes and on the morrow the "word of God" enters the scene. Surprises can be expected. In the section below I reproduce the part of the oracle which comes from the earliest version of the story. The words in italic print provide a key to the oracle's meaning.

> 2 *Samuel* 7
> [4] But that same night the word of the LORD came to Nathan, [5] "Go and tell my servant David, "Thus says the LORD: Would you build me a *house* to dwell in?"
> [11b] Moreover the LORD declares to you that the LORD will make *you a house.*
> [16] "And *your house* and your kingdom shall be made sure for ever before me; your throne shall be established forever."

Reality replaces David's charming personality and inviting humility. The project he proposed had to be evaluated on the basis of its own merits. From God's viewpoint, the construction of a cedar house has never been a high priority. Even if it were desirable, what led David to consider himself as its executor?

The word of God so often reverses human expectations, and this occasion further confirms that notion. As Nathan indicated, this house is not for God; rather, God will make a real "house" for David. What is that house? The Hebrew word for house is *bayit*; it can refer either to a building or to a family. The house in this oracle will be nothing other than a family, with heirs and a perpetual line of progeny. This royal "house," then, includes a "kingdom" and a "throne." The play on the word for "house" gives the prophet's response an ironic twist: expected results will come true in an unexpected fashion. Word plays often evoke laughter, and perhaps Nathan intended David to smile. The king could then have responded: "I almost had it correct, didn't I?!"

For those who look to the Israelite monarchy as a way of experiencing divine guidance, this oracle provides joyful news. David, like Solomon at Gibeon, will receive much more than he had hoped to accomplish! Subsequent Jewish and Christian interpreters have read the text from this vantage point and found in it a firm foundation for messianic expectations. Nathan's word to David thus offers consolation and hope to many people.

In this exploration of the spirituality of the temple, what can Nathan's oracle proclaim about Israel's temple, "the house of God/the LORD"? The LORD's house plays only a minor role in the early story, for those scribes who retold it realized that human security was more important than projects and building security. The real "house" is a family and Israel's storytellers knew that fact. They could remember the story of the midwives who resisted Pharaoh's pressure in Egypt; they received "houses" as the reward for "fear of the LORD" [Exod 1:21]. Those houses were their families, given them because of their courageous preservation of lives in other families.

Many people in our day question government expenditures which implicitly put the constructed house ahead of the human house. Should a government engage in massive armament buildup, or a space program, or monuments if those funds would need to be diverted from crucial human service programs? Nor does the situation in our churches differ radically. Today we must justify monies spent for facilities and aesthetic purposes in the context of growing world hunger and need. But even these reflections move us only a bit closer to the basic problem which arose in the Nathan oracle.

The play on the word "house" forces us to ask where we find God. Is God most present in the shrine, the sanctuary, the building, the poor, the leaders, the whole community? The scribes who transcribed this oracle recognized the tension between project and people which plagues every attempt to discover God's presence in our midst. Many people opt to look for divine presence in a temple, because buildings seem more secure. This brief reminiscence from David's life casts a vote for divine presence and action through persons, and especially through leaders.

A similar ambiguity runs through our own varied conceptions of "church." Is it a building, or a community of people? One can soften the building notion by seeing it as a place to experience divine presence through time. Then the place serves to bond many generations of people together, providing contact with those who precede or who follow us in time. But that mode of presence does not stand on its own; it derives from the people, who provide the real ongoing link. A temple or a church building, it seems, remains an ambivalent symbol of divine presence.

So this narrator offers a qualified view of David's inclination to construct a house for the LORD. The story implies that God's house must always be subordinated to the human house, the human family. The difficulty which we experience while trying to discern divine presence results from a tension like that which Nathan tried to articulate. The builder's way of establishing secure presence, especially for God, falls victim to a joke, a play on words, a tugging at deeper realities, a look at what really constitutes God's presence in Israel: people chosen for relationship, not for a building.

According to Walter Brueggemann, the Nathan oracle is one of those stories which express the "sure truth of the state."[7] Such truth shores up a monopolistic form of government by proposing clear, unambiguous explanations. Such narratives, he notes, end up being poor stories, since they sacrifice imagination for ideology and certitude. Any state or church too concerned about its own preservation demands confidence in the organization's story. But explanatory stories require simple, stereotypical thinking, since the human imagination tends to surface too many questions and too much doubt. One can read this Nathan story in just this way: God has promised a secure house, throne and kingdom to David's family, forever. So sure a promise provides unassailable hope in the type of leadership represented by the king. But another reading, poised on the question of "God's house" in Jerusalem, yields a very different response. The only certainty is the insecurity of David's plans.

The oracle of Nathan, however, provides most Christians with more certainty than ambiguity. An entire tradition reads this as God's promise through Nathan of a Messiah for

---

[7]Walter Brueggemann, *David's Truth*, p. 72.

Israel. Centuries of reflection on its ambiguous meaning have yielded to the easier promise of a messianic savior, which it seems to hold forth. This will prove true for us if we do not hear the distinction between community and building, if we do not continue to feel that unresolved tension in our lives. But if we read this text only within the lens of messianic hope, we encounter another problem. Messianic certainty blocks efforts to hear its radical proclamation: My presence is not in a house you may construct, but in a "house" family which I shall build for you. Even if the "anointed one" belongs to this family sprung from David's loins, Nathan's word focuses on the entire family, the whole community and not just the awaited one. That promise to David incorporates all of us who trace our lineage from him into a "house" of promise and of challenge.

Nathan's oracle does not reject religious attachment to particular places, but it clearly relativizes their importance. An overly Messianic view of God's promise through Nathan in this text has obscured its important critique of the attempt to locate and secure God's presence. This characterization may typify some elements of Catholic tradition, where messianic interpretation of 2 Samuel 7 has led to over-confidence about Christ's accomplishments for us. Fascination with messianic figures may be linked to overly exalted notions of church leaders. Nathan's encounter with David clearly asks us whether we rely too heavily on the abiding promise—"forever"—to David.

At the same time Nathan's words to David invite us to avoid rejecting the building or temple which David wished to construct. If the prophet actually relativizes that type of security, he does not repudiate its value completely. Such a stance emerges in overly-critical religion, occasionally in Protestant circles reacting to counter-problems in Catholicism. For all Christians and Jews, this promise to David relativizes the importance of place and structure for divine presence.

Solomon Executes the Plan

A very different picture emerges in the cycle of Solomon stories in 1 Kings 3-11. The biblical narrative moves from irony and caution about sacred space in David's life to a proud description of the temple constructed by Solomon, his son. We encounter here a broader collection of stories passed down by priests and court writers. They glorify Solomon as builder of the Jerusalem temple.

At the end of the Solomon section, the biblical writers identify a major source which they used in writing their Solomon story. They point to an early source which they had incorporated: "Now the rest of the acts of Solomon, and all that he did, and his wisdom, are they not written in the book of the acts of Solomon" [1 Kgs 11:41]. So "The Acts of Solomon" gave them a starting point, a first optimistic look at the temple construction. The temple stood as the chief monument to the activity and wisdom of King Solomon. This source gave later generations the detailed specifications of the temple building in 1 Kgs 6-7. It also included the Solomonic wisdom stories and led to the view that the temple represented Solomon's greatest act of wisdom. Altheugh the following words probably come from the Deuteronomists, they convey the ancient traditions about the wisdom of Solomon: "the LORD gave Solomon wisdom, as he promised him" [1 Kgs 5:12a]. It was his wisdom that so attracted Hiram king of Tyre to him, and their collaboration resulted in the construction of the temple.

Ancient Voices About the Temple: Designer's Description [1 Kings 6-7]

To understand what kind of records these were, one must imagine the court writers who surrounded Solomon. These were men drafted into service of the great king Solomon to produce documents complimentary to his reign and laudatory of his building projects.[8] The voices of those who suffered under his "levy of forced labor . . . thirty thousand men" [1 Kgs 5:13] certainly have no spokesperson in these texts. Yet Solomon's wisdom, a gift of God to a humble young monarch at Gibeon, develops swiftly. The characterization also depends on other stories: his discerning judgment of the two women in court, his administrative wisdom, and his building projects, including his greatest achievement, the house of the LORD.

The definition of wisdom also undergoes significant changes from one story to the next. The individual voices which we presumed to hear in 1 Kings 3 have been silenced in favor of a calculus of the masses. Wisdom now concerns what seems best for the nation, for the entire Jerusalem government and religious structure. These court-centered

---

[8]One entertaining and perceptive attempt to imagine the writing personnel and process in the Solomonic court is found in an East German novel by Stefan Heym, *The King David Report* (London: Abacus, 1972). Heym depicts the life of a certain scribe named Ethan. He was forcefully enlisted to produce the "King David Report," and often faces the dilemma of presenting facts as his research uncovered them . . .or approving the state's version of it all.

sources do not critique the changing ideology of the monarchy, but they do plant the seeds of a theological reversal in the audience. Solomon's final condemnation in 1 Kings 11 should shock no careful listener.

We turn now to the type of description which the historian left us. We find glimpses of every type of detail of the building's plans and construction in 1 Kings 6-7. The general measurements and division into chambers and rooms can be ascertained from 1 Kings 6:2-10. Any amateur architectural student would enjoy making a sketch from these details. A construction estimator would learn from these plans enough details about types of wood to begin cost estimations. The interior decorations, the furnishing of the sanctuary, the cherubim of the inner sanctuary, the designs carved in the wood—these and other details are described in 1 Kgs 6:15-36. In 1 Kgs 7:13-51 we read about the artistry and construction of the bronze and gold furnishings of the temple complex. The scribes clearly remind us that much of the artistic beauty of the temple came from Phoenicia [1 Kgs 7:13-14].

The long list of artistic vessels and furnishings envisioned for the temple suggests a new trend in Israel. The beauty of created and crafted objects everywhere stands out in this section. This sensibility could certainly emerge in wisdom groups, where the beauties of creation define part of God's relation with the world. In addition, some scholars in comparative religion have studied the type and design of the various furnishings. The molten sea [1 Kgs 7:23-26], the twelve oxen on which it stood [1 Kgs 7:25], the bronze pillars named Jachin and Boaz [1 Kgs 7:15-22], and the cherubim [1 Kgs 6:23-28] all resemble religious symbols and art from neighboring countries. If our stance is critical we will speak of Solomonic syncretism. If, on the contrary, we incline toward an appreciation of wisdom, we may speak of recovering a deeper meaning in non-Israelite symbols. Whatever our judgments, we recognize in Solomon's temple a remarkably open stance toward the world of religious values and symbols. Jerusalem's early writers and signers rejoice in this accomplishment.

Some readers might conclude that this exquisite description of Solomon's temple justifies elaborate church buildings and decorating in our own day. But the texts hardly seem to justify such a naive reading, for they point to the possibility of seeing indications of the divine in all of earth's materials. By extension, the proper object of wisdom inquiry also includes the artistic skills of human workers, even the contributions of foreigners. Solomon's openness to God in unexpected areas of the world does not suit all times, nor all groups of people, to be sure.

The character of Solomon's political development helps to account for the openness of those temple historians and scribes who provide us this account. In a time of expansionism the religious establishment and the court writers do not exercise the same religious restraint which would be needed during times of oppression or defeat. Solomon's reign saw expansionism in political organization, in international relations, in public works projects, in economic prosperity. His religious horizon also expanded, as he allowed foreign elements into the temple, through the doorway from his harem. We find here an unusual religious development in Israel: contrary to their history of rejecting every aspect of worship of other gods, this new moment is characterized by willingness to revalue and transform a multitude of alien symbols. It seems to be a spirituality for a particular moment in Israel, and it finds parallels only at certain discrete times in our day.

Perhaps the openness to the world heralded by Vatican II, particularly in the Pastoral Constitution on the Church in the Modern World, makes far more historical sense when viewed in the light of the Solomonic temple. Both phenomena possess some inherent dangers, and we may suppose that the modern resistance to change in the Roman Catholic Church had a clear counterpart in Solomonic Israel.

Social scientists suggest another way of reading these enthusiastic Solomonic accounts. They may represent the voice of the settled, empowered, bureaucratic classes—both political and religious—which accompanied the growth of the monarchy. We have already noted the upsurge of forced labor required for Solomon's public works project. This social institution amounted to a type of debt-slavery; as such, it was antipathetic in every respect to Israel's own Exodus heritage. Here stands a reminder that the peace and prosperity of some—of those close to the court—cannot stand without reminder of the oppression of others. So the prosperity and openness of Solomonic rule and religion did not characterize everyone at that time. It also is a spirituality for select groups. Social reality plays as much a part in this text as does historical change.

In my mind, the enthusiasm about Solomon's temple and the largely submerged voice of social criticism detected within this text present us with one of the thorniest problems of biblical spirituality. While I have often shifted attention from the ancient text we are considering to contemporary events and then proposed questions for reflection, this method cannot suffice here. In this case the mood of the stories and traditions which one encounters contains the tension between extremely open and closed outlooks on life. If I choose to follow a path of openness and embark on a creation-centered spirituality or a more ecumenical stance toward the rest of my world, I still must admit the presence of those groups for whom enlightenment and openness do not bring any good news. These are the poor and the oppressed, whose concerns become further submerged when other issues take higher stage. So the dilemma proposed to us by the different voices within the text illustrates the complexity of our own world. How can we discern which group we belong to? More importantly, how does my group's concerns and notion of truth affect my own view of self and God and world? Put more starkly, how can a Christian who focuses prophetically on the needs of the poor accept and find nourishment in the self-congratulatory narratives in 1 Kings 3-11?

Any attempt to read only a part of the texts—especially those parts which we find suitable to our tastes—seems to be rejected by the witness of these texts. We who search these texts today for our own faith resources would do well to observe what our forebears did with the traditions they received: they transmitted a variety of voices of God's people. Some groups clearly did not receive equal time in most of the texts, but the variety of positions we observe here must remind us of even greater complexity in Solomonic Israel.

In 1 Kings 6-8 the story implies that not everyone enjoyed the splendor of this temple. Many suffered for its construction; they remind us that ecumenism and openness to all the created world promise blessing only when accompanied by a listening heart, open to discerning the voices of those who do not enjoy the benefits of our spiritual nourishment. The biblical text enshrines no single-issued viewpoint. Rather, the variety which the text offers us provides a lasting memory of past differences. Such divergences in spirituality can only be overcome in the life of the faith community which preserves, honors, and listens to these sacred writings.

Enshrining the Ark in the Temple

Solomon's temple includes many remnants of ancient, non-Yahwistic religions. An Israelite could rightly wonder what compels belief in the LORD's presence there. The religious illustrations, the ancient Canaanite use of cherubim in worship, the structural design patterned after temples in other lands and for other gods all demonstrate Solomon's openness. These aspects, moreover, pose obstacles to association of this building with the God of Israel's life, both past and present.

By comparison, twenty years ago the accumulation of signs, symbols, and statues in many Catholic church buildings posed for many Christians a similar hindrance to prayer and worship focused on Christ or on God. In recent years many of these cluttered buildings have undergone two kinds of changes: removing many superfluous images and decorations, and transferring the tabernacle, which houses the reserved Eucharist, to a special site or room.

An Ancient Temple Dedication: Solomon's Ceremony [1 Kgs 8:1-13]

After the temple building was completed and furnished with those treasures stored up by David [1 Kgs 7:51], it was dedicated by bringing the ark into its innermost section [1 Kgs 8:1-13]. In this narrative a careful reader can discover voices of several eras and groups within Israel, so I will concentrate here on early priestly contributions to the story. Certain elders of Israel and priests gathered in procession to bring the ark, the tent, and the holy vessels from the city of David into this "house" [1 Kgs 8:1, 3]. There they offered sacrifices [v. 5] and then placed the ark in position under the cherubim [vv. 6-8]. Since this narrative reminisces on the priestly view of the ark situated between the cherubim [Exod 25:10-22], its description of the entry ritual probably comes from priestly circles.

The conclusion of this ceremony seems simple by comparison with the decoration details just rehearsed in 1 Kings 7. Words in italics again present important religious symbols.

> *1 Kings 8*
> [10] And when the priests came out of the holy place, a *cloud* filled the house of the LORD, [11] so that the priests could not stand to minister because of the cloud; for the *glory of the LORD* filled the house of the LORD.
> [12] Then Solomon said,
> "The LORD has set the sun in the heavens,
> but has said that he would dwell in thick darkness.
> [13] I have built thee an exalted house,
> a place for thee to dwell in forever."

The liturgical action of the priests [vv. 10-11] stands apart from that of Solomon [vv. 12-13]. In the former, the association of "thick darkness" with the "glory of the LORD" rings true to priestly theology of the wilderness journey, where God's effective presence was discerned by observing the movement of the cloud over the tent of meeting [Exod 40:34-38]. Here in the new "house of the LORD" a similar thick cloud arose from the incense showered in the direction of the inner room. For a new and more settled age the temple could replace the portable tent. The priests of the Jerusalem temple viewed the entrance of the ark as an explanation of divine presence in the temple. This story bolstered their idea of the sacredness of this place of worship.

Solomon's proclamation also manifests a clear spirituality of divine presence. He has incorporated the thick darkness of the priestly tradition in the tent and introduced it into the inner room of the "exalted house" he constructed for the LORD. Here the LORD "dwells" in the darkness, and this prayer uses the same priestly word used in Exodus 40:35 for the cloud's dwelling over the tent. Solomon's proclamation also contains a theology, for he relativizes the power of the sun, divinized by so many of Israel's neighbors: God "has set the sun in the heavens." In this phrase we hear echoes of the priestly hymn celebrating God's creation [Gen 1:1-2:4a]; Solomon proclaims that the LORD has creative power and exercises it even in regard to the sun.

This God, whose presence Solomon celebrates, not only accompanies Israel but also created and maintains all the universe, including those phenomena which others worship. Dwelling here in the temple is a divinity who creates and blesses, saves and redeems. If the decoration in the temple smacks of syncretism, Solomon's address clearly establishes the LORD as God of all. People who cannot avoid contact with other cultures and theologies, this text proclaims, do well to include all of them within their own purview. Solomon's "catholic" tendency in religious matters runs many of the risks so clearly demonstrated by Protestant critique of Roman Catholicism. His inclusion of rival theologies and spiritual emphases in the worship of the temple forces many of us to ask how well we balance ourselves on this tightrope of inclusion.

For a more concrete example, Catholic reservation of the Eucharistic species in its tabernacle offers a similar experience of divine presence in a church building. For some, the Eucharistic procession associated with the feast of Corpus Christi bears more than subtle resemblance to the ark procession of Solomon's story. The yearning for sacramental presence linked to a certain place remains with us today; it may wax less strongly in particular groups and eras, but traditions like this in our biblical text remind us to honor as well as critique inclinations of this type. If such manifestations of piety might seem outmoded to some, there is no justification for their removal. Conversely, this mode of God's presence did not form the center of spirituality for all in Israel, especially the Deuteronomists. So our Scriptures provide sure foundation for those whose spirituality focuses more on hearing the word of God than on sacramental presence. Our ancestors have gifted us with a text which witnesses to ancient difficulties in defining, determining or limiting God's presence.

The issue of "presence" stands out as very significant in the first document of Vatican II, on the Liturgy. There we find concern for the precise modes of Christ's presence in Eucharistic celebration. The conciliar document, like the biblical texts we have observed, preserves several notions of Christ's presence.

Constitution on the Sacred Liturgy #7

To accomplish so great a work Christ is always present in his Church, especially in her liturgical celebrations. He is present in the Sacrifice of the Mass not only in the person of his minister . . . but especially in the eucharistic species. By his power he is present in the sacraments . . . He is present in his word since it is he himself who speaks when the holy scriptures are read in the Church. Lastly, he is present when the Church prays and sings . . .

The council clearly favored one mode of presence, in the eucharistic species. But this notion had been so highly exalted in Roman Catholic piety, that a much stronger focus on the bread of the Eucharist could have been expected. What is remarkable in this statement is its preservation of several modes of presence of Christ in the church. The text allows us to hear several voices of other Christians, some from centuries past, others from different ecclesial groups. For contemporary Catholics, these various modes of presence allow different emphases in their spirituality while denying validity to none of them. Faithful hearing of our scriptures can teach us how to listen to our own church documents as witnesses to the faith of the church.

Conclusion

Finally, we return to the biblical narratives which focus our attention on the temple. Those early texts which provide the focus of this chapter attest to a deeper ambivalence than we expected. The Nathan oracle offered fairly ambiguous support to any temple architect, yet the monarch did not blatantly reject such a localization of divine presence. Rather, its ambivalent message pushed the audience to deeper discernment of sources of God's presence.

When we moved to the Solomonic narratives we found an enthusiastic portrayal of Solomon the temple-builder in the early source. If we recall the ambiguous message of Nathan about David's desire to build a temple, the shift in outlook becomes obvious. The story moves from caution and reserve to optimism. Some real change in attitudes toward the temple has occurred. Finally, the entry of the ark into Solomon's temple demonstrates the way holy symbols effect holiness for a place for many people. More importantly, the ancient sign of divine presence consecrates this new "house" of God and legitimates it, while the new setting expands the theological view of the worshipers. Now Israel serves a God who reigns over creation as well as one who selects and saves a particularly chosen people.

In the next chapter we will encounter Israelite "preaching" on these temple—oriented texts. Their speaking will certainly offer us different perspectives on the question of God's presence. We can expect that they will reduce some of the tension in order to exhort their followers to temple-oriented piety (the Chronicler). At the same time they will present more critical views of the Solomonic project when temple worship has become too casual, or too secure (the Deuteronomists). Their honest reevaluation of the temple's construction will suggest sober reflections about our own relation to church structures and bureaucracies today.

4

ENCOUNTERING THE LORD IN LITURGY: HOMILETIC SPIRITUALITY OF THE JERUSALEM TEMPLE

God cannot be contained—certainly not in a space, nor in a person either. Our examination of God's presence in Israel's institutional leadership, the monarchy, made the person as receptacle of God's presence painfully ambiguous. The early accounts of David's hopes, of temple construction, and of the ark's procession into the temple yielded strangely varying appraisals of our chance of experiencing God there. When Jerusalem priests left descriptions of the temple, the records they left puzzle us: what kind of divinity requires such ornamentation as you would find in Ugarit or in Egypt? Why does this God prefer to appear in natural phenomena rather than in historical and political events? What happened to the old Tent of Meeting from Moses' days? After the return from Exile, some wondered: what kind of temple ministers did we have in ancient days? These and other painful questions challenged later teachers who would attempt to rekindle and contemporize Israel's ancient traditions.

In the kingdoms of Israel and Judah the priestly records, explanations, and directions for the "house of the LORD" did not fully satisfy the people's desires for a viable spirituality. If they had succeeded, Israel's prophets would not have needed to denounce the sins of idolatry among the people. If the priestly cult and Torah had provided sufficient richness, thousands of Israelites might have found Baal worship less tempting. Why did they find the religion of their neighbors so attractive? What led them to incorporate some of the ancient fertility imagery of the temple into their worship and theology? Would the temple have fallen into such disrepair and un-readiness for worship of the LORD that three kings—Jehoash [2 Kgs 12], Hezekiah [2 Kgs 18] and Josiah [2 Kgs 22]— needed to undertake major repair and renewal of the temple? Would worship of nature divinities and neighborly gods at "high places" have flourished so much that the seventh century Deuteronomists needed to recall Judah from its vagaries?

All of these "facts" can be discovered in the biblical books of Samuel and Kings. They represent the untold story of Israel's assimilation of neighboring cultures and religious sensibilities, but an aspect of their history which they would prefer not to parade before their young and their pious. Even if we do not dwell on them, they still point to many forgotten stories about laxity in worship of the LORD, the neglect of the temple, and the disunity of this people. All of these phenomena called forth a major effort for reformation in the seventh century BCE; customarily we call these reformers the Deuteronomists. In this chapter, we will examine their homiletic view of the temple's role, and then compare it with notions from the Chronicler's history. There we will find remnants of fifth-century reflection on the proper role of the temple in Jewish spirituality.

Deuteronomic Spirituality of the Temple

How often have we been advised to rid ourselves of temptation by cutting off the source of the trials? What would you do about a temple which featured fertility symbols, occasional sacred prostitution and other alien ritual? After learning of the growing number of abuses spawned by worship in Jerusalem, you might expect to hear the Deuteronomists reject totally the cult at the Solomonic temple. Although such admonition would seem to fit well their "either-or" view of the religious and moral life, they never offer this advice to the people of Judah. On this point, at least, these preachers call for reformation rather than revolution.

CENTRALIZED WORSHIP [Deuteronomy 12-16]

Earlier I suggested that the books of Samuel and Kings offer a narrative spirituality to accompany the preached spirituality of Deuteronomy. This narrated history illustrates a way to live out Deuteronomy 12-26, the great code for the covenant people. Though the code covers a wide range of issues, it presents an unobstructed view of its temple spirituality in Deuteronomy 12-16. There it focuses on issues of worship, relating them all to the temple. Chapter 12 calls for centralized worship, while chapter 13 admonishes Israel to reject idolatry, and chapter 14 gives regulations for diet and tithes. Finally, chapter 15 and 16 offer revised programs for the annual cycle of festivals.

In effect, Deuteronomy 12 gives the deuteronomic agenda and plan. Israel should destroy the "places" where the nations worship their gods [vv. 2-3], seek "the place" which God will choose for them, and proceed there [v. 5]. There they shall center their faith-life and worship [vv. 6-28]. The following selection from the homily provides its central point, and words in italics suggest important deuteronomic concerns and motifs.

> *Deuteronomy 12*
> [5] You shall seek the *place* which the LORD your God will *choose* out of all your tribes to put his *name* and make his habitation there; thither you shall go,
> [6] and thither you shall bring your burnt offerings and your sacrifices, your tithes and the offering that you present, your votive offerings, your freewill offerings, and the firstlings of your herd and of your flock;
> [7] and there you shall eat before the LORD your God, and you shall *rejoice*, you and your households, in all that you undertake, in which the LORD your God has *blessed* you.

These verses also contain central emphases of deuteronomic spirituality. Israel shall celebrate its festivals with joy, rejoicing at this temple. Later, Deut 16 will direct them to celebrate Passover at the temple, not at home. Their activity at the temple—including also the burnt offerings and the communion sacrifices so carefully described by the priests in Leviticus—all comes together to constitute God's blessing on Israel. Since blessing comes to those who choose to walk in the LORD's covenant paths, the temple and its worship represents the actualization of Israel's covenant relation with the LORD.

The motif of "the place which the LORD (your God) will choose" occurs six times in this chapter: 12:5, 11, 14, 18, 21, 26. Since the composer of the speech takes us back in time to Moses' day, God's choice of a place appears as a future reality ("will choose"). Those, however, who hear this sermon on covenantal fidelity realize that the place has long been designated; it is Jerusalem, with its temple. If Israel would adhere only to this one "place" for worship—instead of going to worship at Judah's high places—their religious unity would result in social-political unity and blessings of *shalom*. And if the audience needs proof that the temple is the correct place, they should remember that it is the one "the LORD chose." The Deuteronomic theologians emphasize God's choice of this place and this people: you can remain the "chosen people" only if you adhere to God's "chosen place" for the centering of your lives. The preachers do not advocate revolutionary new forms and places of worship; rather they passionately exhort Israel to reform its spiritual life, to return to the temple and the LORD.

TOUCHING UP HISTORY FOR THE PULPIT

For a moment, let us return to the narrative theology of the temple in Samuel-Kings. In the previous chapter we pondered the early monarchy's hope and pride in the Jerusalem temple. But the enthusiasm of priests and court scribes never obliterated either the ironic nature of this achievement [2 Sam 7: what kind of "house" will be built?] or the sideways glance at its art and decorations [1 Kgs 6:1-38; 7:13-51] and labor schemes [1 Kgs 5:13-18]. Both aspects were more appropriate for Canaanite temples. The Deuteronomists possessed these stories, with their troubling elements, and they knew other traditions which had been added to them over the centuries, often by prophetic groups. In order to exhort their contemporaries to genuine reform of their lives, the Deuteronomists made further additions to the story which they retold. We shall examine a few of them.

Nathan's Oracle [2 Sam 7:1-17]

Our reflections on the Nathan oracle addressed its ancient nucleus. There we found David's desire to build a house for the LORD transformed into a promise of a house/family for him. In the seventh century BCE, however, Israel's preachers had no doubt that God willed Israel to have a temple. When the Deuteronomists expanded this oracle, they presumed divine approval of the "house of the LORD." They also saw further sources of divine presence in the monarchy and the temple. Following God's promise to build a "house" for David [2 Sam 7:11b], they inserted several verses which interpret Solomon's reign and activity as part of the divine largess to David. Deuteronomic emphases are in italics.

> 2 *Samuel* 7
>
> [12] When your days are fulfilled and you lie down with your fathers, I will raise up your *offspring* after you, who shall come forth from your body, and I will establish his kingdom. [13] He shall build a *house for my name*, and I will establish the throne of his kingdom forever. [14] I will be his father, and he shall be my son. When he commits iniquity, I will chasten him with the rod of men, with the stripes of *humans* (translation mine); [15] but I will not take my *steadfast love* from him, as I took it from Saul, whom I put away from before you.

This preacher pretends to answer the questions that many hearers of the ancient story harbored: why do we need a "house of the LORD" if God told David not to worry about it? The LORD continues the promise to David through his offspring, especially the one who would have a kingdom [v. 12]. This could only be Solomon.

Then the preachers might ask us to imagine God as speaker: "And look what he constructed, 'a house for my name.' This house does not contain me, or confine my dwelling-place. No, within it my name resides, available for speaking and hearing. But you cannot grasp or manipulate my presence for your own desires. This is not the kind of temple you have received." Even Solomon should have learned that he would be punished if he committed iniquity [v. 14]. These preachers hoped their audience would pick up the hints pointing to Solomon's final evaluation [1 Kgs 11:1-13]. Finally the Deuteronomists remind seventh-century worshipers—who must choose between different religious and political factions—that God's steadfast love, the core of covenantal spirituality, can be lost even more easily than received.

In this insertion the preachers use a very different language. They address their audience in the here-and-now instead of the distant past. How have they done this? They speak of the temple which "we have in our day." They demonstrate how Solomon's relation to it came from God, and his role in its construction could be relived by monarchs who care for the upkeep of the building and the purity of its worship. The audience can participate, as did "all the inhabitants of Jerusalem" and "all the people" in the days of King Josiah when he directed the great reform [2 Kgs 23:2].

In fact, the hearers should not expect the ruler to do it all for them—if they had no role, there would be no need for this sermon! Finally, the Deuteronomists reminded them of a resource for the difficult path on which they were called: God's steadfast love. More even than in David's generation, seventh-century Judahites heard much about the covenantal relationship with the LORD. Moses had really introduced them to it, and it came to characterize their spirituality of careful discernment and choosing between life and death.

In our day, can we fail to hear traces of our own church preaching in this ancient homily? What was spoken to David about God's faithful love addresses us also. The house built of humans emerges in our theology of church. The problem of focusing of leadership in a fallible monarch repeats itself continually, especially in churches where the authority of chosen persons stands very highly. The conditionality of it all addresses us very poignantly: we know that the choice is ours, life or death. Our reforming ancestors knew that a God who would enter into a loving covenantal relationship would propose that love be their primary motivation—not fear of legal judgment. The tentative aspect of this relationship affects all these modes of God's presence. Every leader and religious institution stands subordinated to the name and word of God.

Solomon's Temple Building [1 Kings 5-7]

In the previous chapter I did not comment on Solomon's preparations to build the temple and palace in 1 Kings 5:1-12, because it seems to come from deuteronomic writers. But here our concern is with their style of preaching. We find

Solomon discussing his construction plans with Hiram of Tyre; this reasoning reminds us of the "new" version of the Nathan oracle.

> *1 Kings 5*
> [2] And Solomon sent word to Hiram, [3] "You know that David my father could not build a house for the name of the LORD his God because of the warfare with which his enemies surrounded him, until the LORD put them under the soles of his feet. [4] But now the LORD my God has given me rest on every side; there is neither adversary nor misfortune. [5] And so I purpose to build a house for the name of the LORD my God, as the LORD said to David my father, 'Your son, whom I will set on your throne in your place, shall build the house for my name.'"

These preachers found a new reason for Solomon's role in the temple construction: David's reign was too conflicted by hostile forces to allow him the leisure to build a temple. Now that the institution stands, doubt about its appropriateness exits quickly. But loyalty to ancient traditions dies slowly, so the Deuteronomists did what many preachers often do— they alter slightly the meaning of a word or phrase of their text and offer a new meaning. Here they follow the same pattern set in 2 Samuel 7. God's promise about the "house" was only in doubt during David's time, for by now the preachers know it only awaited fulfillment by his son, Solomon. The Deuteronomists interpreted the LORD's promise of a "house" the same way in both passages: "He [Solomon] shall build a house for my name" [2 Sam 7:13a]. Of course, the dialogue with Hiram romanticizes for pious folk a set of negotiations that is more appropriate for business managers.

The Deuteronomists had a penchant for reinterpreting practical, secular events in religious language. If I sound overly critical, I do so only to call attention to our own subtle ways of rereading the past for our own comfort and security. In particular, those who proclaim and preach the word publicly face decisions similar to those of their deuteronomic ancestors. We experience a similar style of reinterpretation with our own family stories. Parents reinterpret as they recount family history to their children, and these same adults will be able to articulate clear principles for retelling biblical stories for children. For example, adults generally omit the wrongdoings of biblical heroes—especially stories with sexual overtones; perhaps they hope not to confuse the child's clear perception of the moral values the adults wish to elucidate. They also present the institutions in which their life is embedded in the most edifying light available, providing a "truth" which children can live by as they mature. So we might judge the efforts of these Deuteronomists less on their fidelity to the bare historical data than on their intention to invite Israel to return to the LORD, with one heart and sensibility, celebrating their chosenness at one place of worship.

The plan for Solomon's temple in 1 Kings 6 contains two deuteronomic comments embedded within it: the date at the beginning, and an oracle to the king in midsection. They indicate the date on which the building of the temple began: "In the four hundred and eightieth year after the people of Israel came out of the land of Egypt, in the fourth year of Solomon's reign . . . " [1 Kgs 6:1]. Commentaries wax eloquently about the chronological problems contained in this notice, but few emphasize the obvious theological point:

this temple project is compared to the Exodus event. The ancient story of God's saving presence to Israel now has a counterpart in the divine presence secured by the construction of a house for the name of the LORD. The liberating traditions of the Exodus have not been replaced, but they now stand in tension with a more orderly divine presence in this "house."

Security cannot be grasped, however, for God alone can grant it through the power of the divine word. The oracle which interrupts the architectural list emphasizes the unpredictability and challenge posed by God's word.

> *1 Kings 6*
>
> [11] Now the *word of the* LORD came to Solomon, [12] "Concerning this house which your are building, if you will walk in my statutes and obey my ordinances and keep all my commandments and walk in them, then I will establish *my word* with you, which I spoke to David your father. [13] And I will dwell among the children of Israel, and will not forsake my people Israel."

The typical focus on "word of the LORD" and "my word" reminds us of the Deuteronomists. Moreover, it views the Nathan oracle as a signal for Solomon to build the temple. Speaking about "statutes and odinances" would also alert anyone who knew Deuteronomy well to the deuteronomic language here.

The well-tuned ear will recognize an exhortation in this oracle. It proclaims that divine presence in this temple is not magically induced: it depends on the obedience of king and people to the stipulations of the covenant. In more personal terms, God will fulfill the promise to build David a "house" only if Solomon faithfully adheres to his relationship with the LORD. I perceive a haunting voice uttering this word right in the midst of a proud listing of building specifications: "its foundations rest on you." Clearly the homilist prepared all Israel to grasp the intent of Solomon's prayer at the temple dedication [1 Kgs 8:14-61]. In addition, all hearers—including us today—must ponder the challenge proposed in God's word. The institutions in which we participate stand only as securely as our fidelity in relations with God and each other.

Introducing the Ark [1 Kgs 8:1-13]

Finally, we observe one small deuteronomic insertion into the story of Solomon's transferral of the ark into the temple [1 Kgs 8:1-13]. While the early priestly writers remarked on God's mysterious and powerful presence, the seventh-century preachers remind their hearers that the power lies not in the symbol but in God's word: "There was nothing in the ark except the two tables of stone which Moses had put there at Horeb, where the LORD made a covenant with the people of Israel when they came out of Egypt" [1 Kgs 8:9]. We have moved from the numinous, powerful, saving presence of the LORD Sabaoth, represented by the ark, to a religious symbol replete with deuteronomic theology. We now have an "ark of the covenant of the LORD" [1 Kgs 8:1], instead of the older "ark of God". This ark brings to fruition the ancient Exodus traditions.

This homiletic presentation of presence in the temple restricts our penchant for concretizing God's presence in the ark. Conversely, it exercises a typical "catholic" strategy of including all traditions and sensibilities in one overarching symbol, the Jerusalem temple. So the ardent preachers of one

God and one place of worship spread their wings wide enough to encompass every group that does not express hostility to the worship of the LORD. Here we may recognize the blessing of a catholic approach to various spiritualities; the inclusion of all allows strong focus on the one center of focus and prayer.

A SPIRITUALITY FROM LITURGICAL PRAYER: SOLOMON AND THE TEMPLE [1 Kings 8]

These deuteronomic additions to the ancient narratives subtly point toward a very special theology of the Jerusalem temple and its worship. They demonstrate the quality and style of an authentic temple spirituality. But the Deuteronomists also inserted a marvelous example of their spirituality when they recreated Solomon's speech and prayer at the liturgy of the dedication of the temple [1 Kgs 8:14-53].

The early temple traditions include a priestly story in which the ark was settled in the holy place and Solomon uttered a brief song of praise [1 Kgs 8:12-13]. The next part of this ceremony echoes a very different voice and liturgical setting. In the rest of the chapter Solomon leads the people in worship, so neither priests nor Levites appear again. It all begins with the king's speech to the people [1 Kgs 8:14-21], after which follows his long dedication prayer [1 Kgs 8:22-53]. Both actions take place before "all the assembly of Israel." During the speech, the people stand and Solomon faces them [1 Kgs 8:14]; during the prayer he stands before the altar—probably facing the same direction as the

people—with his hands spread towards the heavens [8:22].
Both gestures convey a profound liturgical spirituality.

Solomon's speech to the people begins with a typical
formula, "Blessed be the LORD, the God of Israel" [1 Kgs
8:15]. It continues with a recounting of God's gracious acts
toward Israel, all of which invite this praise and worship.
God fulfilled the promise to David in two ways: by the
dynasty carried on through his son Solomon [v. 20], and by
the construction of this temple [vv. 20-21]. Both gifts had
been promised through Nathan [2 Sam 7:13ff]. He recalls
the LORD's word to David about his plan to build a temple,
"you did well that it was in your heart" [v. 18b]. The earlier
doubt about God's will for the temple has submerged. The
LORD desired this place, and David, too; so it could become
the "house for the name of the LORD." The concluding line
about the temple contains clear deuteronomic theology:
"there I have provided a place for the ark, in which is the
covenant of the LORD which he made with our fathers,
when he brought them out of the land of Egypt" [v. 21].
Suddenly the ark reappears, but not as the numinous power
or force which used to accompany Israel into battle in the
holy war. This ark represents Israel's covenant relationship
with the LORD. This place and this ark concretize the
covenantal relationship mediated by Moses between God
and Israel in Sinai. The promise to David really brings to
completion the ancient covenant with Moses.

We may find little that surprises us in this speech, for we
easily harmonize traditions about Moses and David into a
single theological stream. By doing this we act in a very
"catholic" fashion, where uniting all the traditions wears
down the special features that make each of them distinctly

fresh. For example, reading the Jewish Scriptures as "preparation for the New Testament" acts as a self-fulfilling prophecy about what religious and spiritual value we shall find there. We may bypass whatever does not point towards the Christian Scriptures. For seventh-century Judahites, the promise inherent in Nathan's word to David would be tempered by the need to make choices in the Mosaic covenant tradition. When these preachers affirm that God willed the temple's construction, they shift the area of uncertainty from the identity of the "house" to the behavior of the people. Exhortation to personal renewal and reform rests not on ambiguous promises but on clearly defined choices. Those who prefer to discover God's presence in the story of their lives will not gravitate to deutoronomic exhortations.

Solomon's prayer is long and complicated, like many liturgical prayers which develop over time. Its introduction addresses God and articulates the position and hopes of the one who prays [1 Kgs 8:22-26]. Next, it reflects on God's mode of presence. Is it in this temple, and if so, how [1 Kgs 8:27-30]? A final section describes seven concrete cases when prayer in this "house" is appropriate. These situations describe what the people should expect from God when they pray here, or toward this place [1 Kgs 8:30-53]. Taken together, these sections almost present a creed for Israel.

Solomon's opening prayer addresses God not as creator or as cosmic deity (which might fit the building design), but as the "God of Israel . . . guarding the covenant . . . and . . . steadfast love to thy servants" [1 Kgs 8:23]. He reminds God how the promise to David (from God's mouth) has been fulfilled in his son, Solomon (by God's hand) [1 Kgs 8:24]. A petition ends this short collect: confirm your promise to

David about a dynastic family, provided that the people walk in God's paths [1 Kgs 8:25]. When he returns again to the divine word, God should be suitably motivated: "let thy word be confirmed, which thou hast spoken to thy servant David" [1 Kgs 8:26]. Certainly some can recognize here a prayer of gratitude for the status quo, that our past history of God's graciousness toward us be continued through our worship in this structure (temple in Israel, synagogue for Judaism, church for Christianity). While the king does not praise security, this prayer could result in the complacency of those who look for God in old structures.

In case anyone cherishes security in this house of the name of the LORD, Solomon's questions provide a jolt.

> *1 Kings 8*
> [27] But will God indeed dwell on the earth? Behold, heaven and the highest heaven cannot contain thee; how much less this house which I have built!

The temple is *not* the LORD's dwelling place. The reason for this denial does not appear explicitly in the prayer, but when we hear what is important for the prayer leader, we can determine what aspects of temple life are omitted. In his petition to God Solomon begs the LORD to harken to the "supplication of thy servant and of the people Israel, when they pray toward this place" [1 Kgs 8:30a]. Nothing has been mentioned about sacrifices and incense of any kind. Then comes a startling conclusion: "when thou hearest, forgive" [1 Kgs 8:30b]. It takes us by surprise, since repentance had not seemed part of the prayer. Deuteronomic theology of prayer shines forth here, for Israel's need of forgiveness colors all prayer to God. Moreover, the priestly regulation about sin-offerings and sacrifices in the temple disappears from this model prayer of the Deuteronomists. For them, forgiveness comes when God hears the prayer of Israel.

The longest section of this prayer also feels a bit repetitive. Solomon recounts seven concrete situations in which Israel might turn toward the temple to address God. Each time he repeats the same petition to God: "then hear thou in heaven and act" [though there are minor variations, this formula appears in 8:32, 34, 39, 43, 45, 49-50]. A succinct example follows, with key phrases highlighted in italic type.

> *1 Kings 8*
> [35] When heaven is shut up and there is no rain because they have sinned against thee, if they pray toward *this place*, and acknowledge thy name, and turn from their sin, when thou dost afflict them, [36] then *hear thou in heaven and forgive* the sin of thy servants, thy people Israel, when thou dost teach them the good way in which they should walk; and grant rain upon thy land, which thou has given to thy people as an inheritance.

They need rain desperately. The drought results from their sin, and so fits clearly into the covenantal theology in Deuteronomy 30:15-20: choose life and good, or death and evil. But the curse is not final; rather it invites Israel to address God by name, to turn toward the temple, to repent and to cry out for forgiveness and salvation.

God, on the other hand, must pay attention to this prayer and "grant them compassion in the sight of those who carried them captive, that they may have compassion on them" [1 Kgs 8:50]. But why should God display such compassion? Because they are "thy people and thy heritage" brought out of Egypt [1 Kgs 8:51]. God separated them "from among all the peoples of the earth . . . as thou didst declare through Moses thy servant" [1 Kgs 8:53]. The LORD must remain true to the word proclaimed through Moses; the prophetic word cannot fail. More importantly, God's relationship with this people was established in their election, and the strings of affection cannot be so easily discarded. Divine compassion in this text is expressed by the same Hebrew root [*rachamim*] as the narrator used to describe the emotion of the woman who displayed genuine maternity in court before Solomon [1 Kgs 3:16-28]. Such compassion should characterize the LORD as much as this woman! Compassion, moreover, includes and presupposes forgiveness. How could God act otherwise to Israel, chosen to be God's own people?

What kind of deuteronomic spirituality emerges from this dedicatory speech and prayer ascribed to Solomon? Several points surface. First, the life of worship focuses on the temple, but not as a place of sacrifice. Although the sacrificial system is presumed [cf. Solomon's copious sacrifices at the dedication; 1 Kgs 8:62-64], the historians do not focus on this aspect of worship in the temple. One will need to consult other sources for details. Second, deuteronomic spirituality calls upon Israel as a community to focus on "this place," the temple, as its place of prayer and supplication. God's presence there subsists in the "name of the LORD," which begins and closes this prayer. This prayer, of course, provides a model for other prayers. As a model of liturgical prayer, it encompasses the entire community, monarch as well as people. Third, Israel should pray concretely in its petitioning, focusing its needs for a God who hears and harkens. This type of prayer differs from the hymnic praise of many psalms which derive from temple worship. Those hymns often praise God in expansive, cosmic terms without focus on specific human needs. This prayer in the temple focuses on Israel's history and covenant; perhaps it acts as a critique of parts of the psalter.

The deuteronomic spiritualization of the temple may have some parallels today. In Catholic liturgical reform the renewed focus on the Liturgy of the Word aims at balance in a liturgical life that had overemphasized the ritual and sacrificial aspects of worship. A new appreciation of the presence of Christ in groups gathered for prayer has helped many people, especially in charismatic prayer groups, to rediscover the possibility of crying out to God in very specific and particular situations. Both of these contemporary developments have a spiritual ancestry in the Deuteronomists. Finally, the Catholic ritual for the dedication of a church offers one biblical reading from this dedication prayer of Solomon [1 Kgs 8:22-23, 27-30]. Interestingly, its emphasis falls on the temple as place of prayer rather than as dwelling-place of God. This choice of verses for a contemporary liturgical rite interprets liturgical space as gathering-place for prayer rather than as God's dwelling-place. Practically speaking, this subtle change in horizon allows us to evaluate our own sensitivities as we prepare for worship, especially in the Eucharistic liturgy. Some favor personal, private communication with God, while others more readily pray with the others gathered for prayer. Solomon's prayer suggests that when we prepare for Eucharist the needs and cares of all stand on a par with private experience of the sacramental presence of Christ.

The Chronicler's Spirituality of the Temple

After the return from Exile in the sixth century BCE, the Jewish community never was able to recover its energy and rebuild the temple in the splendid fashion of Solomon's construction. Some of the returnees remembered the ancient edifice, so they could only weep when they gazed on its paltry replacement. Of course, there were good reasons for their failure to match the grandeur of Solomon's temple. The gloomy financial situation of the community prevented lavish outlays; combined with this was Judah's political subordination to the Persian empire. But the political and economic explanations do not fully explain their hesitation over the project. Religious hesitation or discouragement must have played its part, so the prophet Haggai's oracles mandating reconstruction of this house of worship attempt to provide a word of God to bolster their energy. The results, however, were far from satisfactory.

FOCUSING ALL OF LIFE ON THE TEMPLE

Into this setting of Judean complacency and hesitation over temple worship, the Chronicler injects an exhortation to return to their center of worship during the monarchy. We have already seen how this preacher refocused spirituality on the king as a spiritual leader by rewriting Israel's history (Chapter Two). Here we find fifth-century preaching exhort faithful participation in the liturgical life of the Jerusalem temple. First, we consider David's transferral of the ark into Jerusalem. Although the Chronicler does not describe the temple in this liturgy of the ark, he carefully includes lists of later temple personnel within the older story. These lists helped priests and Levites of post-exilic Judah to refocus their own identity and roles. Second, David arranged the worship when they arrived in the city, suggesting a sophisticated liturgical sensibility on the part of the Chronicler. Third, a simple change in the Nathan oracle suggests how strongly this homilist of Israel's traditions felt about the temple and its personnel. Finally, the Chronicler views David as the real founder of the temple. He wants to associate Israel's greatest religious institution with its pre-eminent ruler.

The Levites [1 Chronicles 15-16, 23, 25-26]

Just as the narratives of the early monarchy did not fully satisfy the Deuteronomists, so too the robust story of 2 Samuel needed embellishment for the Chronicler's community. The Chronicler transforms an exuberant parade with the ark into a grand liturgical procession, replete with all the ranks of priests and Levites. He even inserts texts of the hymns which they chanted [1 Chr 15:1—16:36]. We learn about Levites, who alone were required to carry the ark [1 Chr 15:2, 13, 15]. The Chronicler also provides several Levitical lists [1 Chr 15:5-10; 15:16-24; 16:4-6], presumably so that Levites of the author's era could be comforted by their legitimation in the sacred story. Although they had not been present in the older story, the Chronicler assures them that their roles existed from ancient times: "the Levites carried the ark of God upon their shoulders with the poles, as Moses had commanded according to the word of the LORD" [1 Chr 15:15]. The historian assigns this important duty to the Levites, whose status receives new strength here.

The Levites had other responsibilities as well. They had charge of music and singing in the sacred procession [1 Chr 15:16-24], and they received specified roles for liturgical prayer before the ark of the LORD "to invoke, thank, and to praise the LORD, the God of Israel" [1 Chr 16:4]. Since these three verbs describe the basic modes of prayer in psalms of Lament, Thanksgiving and Hymns of Praise, we find the Levites entrusted with Israel's sacred song as well as its music, while the priests cared for sacrifice and trumpet blowing.

The Chronicler focuses on the Levites so that they could claim their identity. This careful legitimizing of the Levites satisfies a basic human craving for meaning through external words and events. Similar motives in later generations have led some Catholics to search for biblical texts which concretely link ordained ministry with the life and mission of Jesus. In more recent times an analogous situation emerges as women have sparked study of biblical texts in order to discover their roots and find biblical warrants for their participation in ministerial and leadership roles. On a wider level, the Chronicler's care to inject the Levites into the scene reminds us of a yearning to find ourselves included in some way in the sacred texts which nourish our spiritual life. This proves true especially for groups which find themselves to be regarded as inferior or of secondary importance. For all who feel disenfranchised, the Chronicler's inclusive tendency offers hope for legitimation of their role and identity. Since these texts constitute part of our sacred story, such desires on our part should not be waived as self-seeking; no, the yearnings themselves receive support from this preacher!

These Levitical genealogies [1 Chr 23, 25, 26] also offer identity in a family. Like the yearning which leads many of us today to rediscover our family trees, Levites conducted similar searches. One benefit of such identity building comes from the expansion of our horizons across time. Many contemporary genealogies are kept by religious groups— Mormons for the purpose of rebaptism, Catholics for the purpose of annual prayer for their deceased—so the Chronicler's instincts find a modern parallel. We recognize the twofold function of these genealogies: first, to incorporate oneself within a living group for purposes of identity, and second, to experience communion with others who are separated both by space and time. The Chronicler guarantees the authenticity of such nourishment for those who so hunger.

David as Liturgist [1 Chronicles 15-16]

Finally, the Chronicler's David is liturgist of renown. As he recasts the traditions of 2 Samuel, this writer alters the description of David's appearance as he leads the ark into the city. Following the Levites, "David was clothed with a robe of fine linen, as also were all the Levites . . . and the singers . . . and David wore a linen ephod" [15:27]. Instead of a loincloth as in the older story, David appears dressed like the high priests of the later generation. What else would be appropriate for a king who leads Israel in procession into Jerusalem? Finally, after the ark has come to rest inside the tent, David offers sacrifices, blesses the people, and distributes food to everyone present [1 Chr 16:1-3]. Later, he arranges all of the Levites and priests for a grand liturgical celebration:

"on that day David first appointed that thanksgiving be sung to the LORD by Asaph and his brethren" [1 Chr 16:7]. The Chronicler affirms that the proper prayer type for this liturgy is thanksgiving, and this spirituality of gratitude for divine presence in a holy place remains with us to this day.

Even here the Chronicler teaches his generation how to pray. To this ark processional he adds a song of gratitude composed from various thanksgiving psalms [Ps 105:1-15; Ps 96:1-13; Ps 106:1, 47-48]. This practice of praying psalms communally remains until our day, not only in the weekly worship of churches and synagogues, but especially in the daily prayer life of Jews, and of many Christians, especially in monastic communities. David's choice of psalm texts also reminds us of the importance of choosing psalms appropriate to the events of the day or to the situations of the community. The Chronicler's selections contain significant spiritual motifs: covenant [16:16-17], the glory of the temple [16:27], and thanksgiving ("O give thanks to the LORD, for he is good; for his steadfast love endures forever" [1 Chr 16:34, citing Ps 118:1]). The Chronicler challenges us to prepare liturgical prayer with similar care.

Novelty in Nathan's Oracle [1 Chr 17:1-15]

In the Nathan Oracle to David [2 Sam 7:1-17; 1 Chr 17:1-15] the later historian follows the sacred story from 2 Samuel very closely. But several slight changes suggest God's unequivocal authorization of the monarchy and of Solomon. When Nathan gives the divine question to David, "would you build me a house to dwell in" [2 Sam 7:5], the Chronicler makes it a statement: "You shall not build me a house . . . " [1 Chr 17:4]. Is there a difference? In the older story one wonders if temple building itself will be allowed. After the Exile no one questions the legitimacy of the temple, so it seems to mean "you, David" will not build that house for me. And if not you, then who? Solomon, of course. A simple change in the text makes a profound difference in meaning: it is not a question about the edifice (and all it represents) but about the builder. The Chronicler expresses certainty about the institution, though not about each person. For us a similar tendency arises when we recognize the community's ability to fill some of the voids created by personal inadequacies; the old Latin saying, *ecclesia supplet* ("the church provides") what is lacking in the minister or the situation, aptly describes modern spirituality in this tradition.

David and the Temple [1 Chronicles 22-29]

Finally, we turn to the Chronicler's unusual addition to the David story, his relationship to the Jerusalem temple [1 Chr 22-29]. The book of Samuel recognized only a desire on David's part to build a "house of cedar" for the LORD. It took clever interpretation to legitimate Solomon's construction of the temple as an outcome of God's promise to David. But the Chronicler directly credits the temple to David by putting the planning and preparation for the temple into his hands. Solomon simply carries out the program begun by his father.

The Chronicler must justify this bold change, which he does through retelling of a narrative. David purchases Araunah's threshing floor in 2 Samuel 24. In the ancient source, David purchased this site after his census of Israel had aroused God's ire. As a result, God told David to choose one of three terrible punishments, and when the people were dying of the pestilence, the prophet Gad instructed the king to erect an altar to the LORD on the threshing-floor of Araunah. David obeyed so "the LORD heeded supplications for the land" [2 Sam 24:25] and lifted the plague. But why would the Chronicler retell a story in which David is at fault, since this is the same preacher who totally omits the human face of David in 2 Samuel 11-20? Let us see how the Chronicler's version suits a temple-oriented community.

In 1 Chronicles 21, David prays with liturgical gestures. When he saw the angel of death standing next to the threshing-floor, "David and the elders fell on their faces" and then uttered the same prayer that was found in 1 Samuel [1 Chr 21:16]. Like the old tradition in 1 Samuel, God stays the sword of death from Israel. The following addition, however, supports temple worship in the preacher's own day: "Then David said, 'Here shall be the house of the LORD God and here the altar of burnt offering for Israel'" [1 Chr 22:1]. According to the Chronicler, the temple rests on the site of Araunah's/Ornan's threshing-floor. This preacher proclaims that God pointed out this site to David through an angel. The location is no human invention. Moreover, this temple stands on a spot symbolic of God's compassion for David. Temple prayer for forgiveness of sins, then, comes as no surprise or innovation to the audience of the Chronicler. The Chronicler also suggests an important dimension of sorrow and repentance to the prayer of our public worship.

The Chronicler craftily connects David's life and the site

of the temple. So David proceeds to charge Solomon to build God's house [1 Chr 22], suggesting that he is worthy to do it because "he shall be a man of peace" [1 Chr 22:9]. Peace of course, is a meaning of Solomon's name in Hebrew, and even the children will remember this preacher's flourish! The temple built by Solomon stands as a place of peace and in times of distress signals Israel's yearning for peace.

In the following chapters, we find David setting up and arranging the personnel of post-exilic Israel. First he provides for the temple: the Levites [1 Chr 23], the priests [1 Chr 24], the musicians [1 Chr 25], the gatekeepers, treasurers, and other functionaries [1 Chr 26]. Then he arranges the civil and military orders for his people, implying that fifth-century Israel should be interested not only in the temple, even though their freedom in political affairs was severely limited. He repeats publicly his choice of Solomon to construct the temple and hands over the builder's plan for it [1 Chr 28]. All the while this "history" has a moral to it. The assembly should "observe and seek out all the commandments of the LORD your God" [1 Chr 28:8], while the ruler must "serve [the God of your father] with a whole heart and a willing mind" [1 Chr 28:9]. Once the temple clergy and helpers were established, David points to Solomon as his successor and executor of these projects [1 Chr 29:1-9].

If you have read these long lists of temple ministers, you might find yourself both exhausted by the effort and skeptical about their intent. In their enthusiasm to explain the roles of temple personnel through the lists, these early scribes might seem to provide more evidence for their own legitimation than for knowledge of God. From the history of the Christian church we know that leaders and teachers often spend more energy verifying clerical status and functions than proclaiming God's word. In like fashion, early records from the temple and court often tend to legitimate institutional arrangements, so it seems proper to ask how they provided genuine resources for people searching to respond to God's word.

In this context, the Chronicler offers us some possible reflections. In an era of political impotence, the Chronicler seizes upon the sole arena of Jewish life which allowed his contemporaries to experience and celebrate their identity: the religious sphere, centered around the temple. While the lists of names might seem self-serving, they may also witness to a profound desire for explicit inclusion in this people, through these public lists. Once he has established ministry in the temple as legitimate, the Chronicler includes civic and military personnel almost as a deliberate afterthought. Viewing the province of Judah through the lens of the ancient, divinely directed kingdom of Israel offers hope of a better future to Jews who hear this message. At the same time, the preacher refrains from presenting an explicit message which could involve grave political repercussions for his people. If we wish to understand the Chronicler's subtlety and restraint, we need to imagine church life under alien, repressive political structures. There the issues of survival better compare with the Chronicler's setting.

David's Farewell Prayer [1 Chr 29:10-19]

Finally David prayed a beautiful farewell prayer, in which he articulated the lofty theology of the Chronicler's age [1

Chr 29:10-19]. I would urge you to read this entire prayer slowly and reflectively, for it also expresses a spirituality which this homilist found in David's life and for which he invites his own community to strive with all their heart. One particular point of David's prayer stands out for me, for it seems to embrace the Chronicler's meaning for the temple. The special clause is highlighted in italic: "But who am I, and what is my people, that we should be able thus to offer willingly? *For all things come from thee, and of thy own have we given thee*" [1 Chr 29:14]. David recognizes that everything is gift from God, even the gift of life itself. This temple simply represents a gift to God in return: whatever they offer to God comes from God's gifts to them. The temple, the worship, all the people who minister there—all were desired and designed by God, and symbolize Israel's gift in return to the LORD. For that generation of Jews the temple represents their response to the psalmist's question: "What shall I render to the LORD for all his bounty to me" [Ps 116:12]. For us, then, the temple, the church, even individual church buildings can acquire a meaning of spiritual depth. Each of these institutions may comprise one way of returning to God everything that we have been given by our compassionate God.

Conclusion

In this chapter we have listened to selections from two sets of preachers, the Deuteronomists and the Chronicler. Vastly different religious, political, and social realities confronted their respective congregations, so we have seen how each of them reinterprets ancient temple traditions for their own day. During the monarchy the deuteronomic message proclaimed the God-given aspect of the temple as the realization of Nathan's oracle to David. It subtly called for a shift in emphasis in temple worship, from heavy emphasis on sacrificial rituals to an experience of prayer to the LORD in this house of God's name. Focusing on the temple as the sole place of worship led them to curtail worship of the LORD at high places. These seventh century Deuteronomists pursued a different goal than some of the priests. They offered a religious focus which could unite disparate groups in Judah, where they faced the serious Assyrian threat.

During the Persian era, the Chronicler likewise addressed a somewhat demoralized Jewish community with a vision of temple-oriented religious identity. While the Chronicler's message built on the splendid authority of David's rule, it intended to provide Jews after the Exile with prayerful access to God and hope for some kind of Davidic reign in their future. These two sets of preachers, the Deuteronomists and Chronicler, discerned in the Jerusalem temple a better means of access to God than in the monarchy. These ancestors of ours remind us that authentic spirituality often directs us to face the limitations of our situation and there to discern the best possible response to God's call.

Part III

The Word of God

The history of prophecy in Israel is more difficult to picture than the other institutions we have discussed. Unlike the personnel of the temple, mediators of the word of God had no building whose construction and destruction we can date and describe. Nor have we a history of the prophets, as we have for the kings in Israel and Judah. Temple worship and monarchy had their memorials—temple and palace—but the prophets ministered and then died after a relatively brief span of time. The only shrine left from the prophetic movement was the written record of the word of God which they mediated to Israel.

The prophetic books form a major section of the Hebrew Scriptures. The prophets which Christians know best and cherish are the writing prophets, like Isaiah, Jeremiah, Ezekiel, Amos and Hosea. Each of these prophets speak to us even today through their books, which we find in the canon of our Bibles. Those books are not verbatim reports of the speeches given by the prophets; their followers and disciples probably collected their oracles, edited them and left their collections as a great legacy for later generations. In those books and others—including all of the minor prophets—we hear God's word mediated to Israel, and also to us.

We have not adequately studied prophecy even if we have read and pondered all these prophetic books, and reflected on the prophets who inspired them. Many of us customarily identify prophecy in Israel with the books named after these prophets. To limit prophecy to those books is a disservice to the prophetic movement in Israel. We must look further, to the historical books which form the subject of this study.

The Jewish designation of the different groups of books in their Scriptures proves very helpful for our understanding of prophecy. They call the books named after prophets the Latter Prophets. The books which we have been discussing—in fact, all of the books included in the so-called Deuteronomic History—are called the Former Prophets in their canon. This manner of referring to them seems strange if we view them basically as histories of the monarchy. But we have learned that this so-called history contains much preaching and theological reflection, so we know that it contains far more than political history.

The Jewish view of these books as prophetic alerts us to another aspect of their contents. It invites us to search out the prophetic figures in these books, to examine their roles and to ponder the messages which they delivered. These books actually provide an excellent narrative source for our own understanding of the great writing prophets. The prophets are major actors in this history of Israel during the monarchy, and their activities permeate the narratives of these books. The spiritual vision of these books owes much to the prophets who articulated God's word for commoner and royalty alike. Indeed, calling these books the Former Prophets probably makes more sense than referring to them as the Historical Books.

Nor is prophecy in the Hebrew Bible confined to these books of the Former and Latter Prophets. It extends back to Israel's earlier history, for we find scattered prophetic details in the books of Genesis, Exodus, Numbers, and Deuteronomy. There we find Abraham, Miriam, and Moses described as prophetic persons. In the Book of Genesis, God refers to Abraham as a prophet when advising Abimelech, king of Gerar to return Sarah to her husband. God says to him: "Restore the man's wife; for he is a prophet,and he will pray for you and you shall live" [Gen 20:7]. In this early story the prophet's role was to mediate prayerfully with God for the life of another.

In the Book of Exodus, after God led Israel out of Egypt "Miriam, the prophetess, the sister of Aaron, took a timbrel in her hand; and all the women went out after her with timbrels and dancing" [Exod 15:20]. Here we meet another prophetic role: the prophetess sings a prayer of thanksgiving to God, and accompanies it with dancing. We shall also find that the later preachers of Israel—in 1-2 Chronicles—also envisioned liturgical music, song, and dance as prophetic actions.

Although we do not often think of Moses as a prophet, it is another of the roles he plays in these books. While Israel was wandering in the desert Moses faced a rebellion by Miriam and Aaron, his brother and sister. When they lodge their charge, they ask: "Has the LORD indeed spoken only through Moses? Has he not spoken through us also?" [Num 12:2]. Their complaint against him suggests that he arrogated all prophetic authority to himself. In Chapter Six we shall find other hints of Moses' prophetic role in the books of Exodus, Numbers, and Deuteronomy.

In the Former Prophets, the prophetic figures who stand out from the others are Samuel, Nathan, Elijah, and Elisha. Each of these will find a place in our discussion. Two prophetesses also mediate God's word in special ways in these books. Huldah lived in the seventh century, during the time of King Josiah; we shall meet her in Chapter Six. Deborah, in the Book of Judges, stands as a first prophetic figure in these books. When Israel faced almost certain defeat by Sisera, they "cried to the LORD for help" against him [Judg 4:3]. God's response to Israel's outcry came in the person of this woman. The story continues: "Deborah, a prophetess, the wife of Lappidoth, was judging Israel at the time" [Judg 4:4]. She was responsible for saving the people. Since the Book of Judges usually calls Israel's saviors "judges", it has preserved that title for her while not omitting mention of her prophetic identity. This prophetess managed to defend Israel after they turned and cried out to God. We shall find that the prophets often play this role—bringing God's word of response when Israel cries out in need or oppression. Moses, Elijah, and even a Levitical prophet in 2 Chronicles offer this ministry.

Among the major writing prophets I shall mention Jeremiah, who prophesied at the end of the monarchy in Judah. He viewed Israel's national, cultural and religious history as a continual exercise in deafness to the word. As we shall see, God's word comes also in covenant and in Torah. This prophet castigated his fellow Israelites for failing to abide by their covenant with God and its concrete stipulations for their life. Jeremiah's charge against the people of Jerusalem pinpoints his complaint: they refused to listen to God's prophets, who proclaimed the word of God to them

[Jer 7:25-26]. Their refusal to hear God's word relates directly to their unwillingness to live up to their covenantal relationship. Jeremiah and the Deuteronomists considered Torah as God's plan for their lives, the concrete aspects of the covenant which they had with the LORD. Refusal to live by Torah, then, is a rejection of God's word of Torah mediated through the prophets. Finally, we shall discover that this marriage of prophecy and Torah brings us right back to Moses, the prophet whose shadow extends through all the books contained among the Former Prophets.

The goal of Part Three will be to describe the spirituality of those who mediate and those who hear the word of God. We will focus on significant moments when God's word addressed Israel at the very core of its life. We shall note how leaders and people respond when royal traditions and spirituality of the temple failed to provide guidance and hope. These prophetic texts may help us to answer some of the questions which other prophets, in other books of the Bible, have inspired in us. How did they recognize God's word? Where did it come from ? How effective was it? What hope and challenge does God's word in Israel provide for our day?

In these books, I seem to discover two different sources for God's word. In the prophetic encounters (often with the monarchs of Israel) and oracles, God's voice speaks through clearly narrated incidents. These stories and oracles invite us to enter into some of the most poignant narratives about Israel's life, where the word of God forms part of narrative spirituality for those who hear and those who speak that word.

For the Deuteronomists, prophets play two roles. First,

they mediate God's saving word for Israel, just as Moses had done long before. Second, they challenge Israel to live according to Torah, God's word revealed to them for their life in the Land. The Chronicler, on the other hand, introduces the prophetic spirit and the living word of God among the Levites, lively and courageous temple ministers of his own day. In these two traditions we find a homiletic spirituality of the word of God. They exhort their contemporaries to hear God speaking to them through Torah and through temple worship and its ministers. They also challenge us to listen carefully for the word of God addressing us in our own day.

5

PROPHETS AS SPEAKERS
OF GOD'S WORD:
NARRATIVE SPIRITUALITY OF
THE WORD OF GOD

Most stories about prophetic proclamations of God's word occur at critical points in Israel's history. They often concern leadership among the people and the foreign affairs of the two kingdoms, Israel and Judah. The prophetic word serves to legitimate rulers or to lay judgment on them, but it also calls the entire people to move beyond their own powers of analysis, prediction, and action to a new vision. Many of these stories can be identified as sagas or legends, more ancient than the deuteronomic history in which they now appear. We look to stories such as these when we attempt to discern a narrative spirituality of the prophetic word of God.

In this chapter I will invite you to hear God's word spoken by prophets in three different kinds of situations. First, some prophets articulate God's design for social and institutional change. Sometimes this need requires them to reject those in Israel—especially its leaders—whose lives do not serve to build up *shalom* for the people. Second, prophets often address God's life-sustaining word to the crucial issues of daily life and subsistence, such as famine, property rights, and death of loved ones. The word which the prophets mediate affects the entire fabric of Israelite society. Third, Israel's prophets arose as mediators of God's word during the era of the monarchy. They often designate new leaders either by word or by gesture. Just as emphatically do they reject kings who do not observe the covenant.

Key stories about prophets demonstrate two significant patterns. First, prophets utter God's word to reject unworthy and useless leaders and institutions; in turn, they often introduce or designate their replacements. For example, at the beginning of the Samuel story an unnamed prophet utters an oracle of doom against the priestly house of Eli [1 Sam 2:27-36]. This occurred at a time when Israel's social and religious fabric had almost completely deteriorated. Second, the word of God speaks personally to the young Samuel [1 Sam 3], calling him to ministry, eventually replacing Eli's priestly family. The prophetic word of God rejected the unworthy leader, and then established a new, authentic leader. These two narratives in 1 Samuel offer one pattern of prophetic involvement in Israel.

The second pattern emerges when prophets speak and act for the people in times of great need. Prophets often address a word of God to people who are suffering, especially those who face life-threatening dangers. For example, when Elijah understood the impact of the drought on the widow of Zarephath, he uttered a word of God which provided sustenance for her and her son. In stories of this type, the prophets often remind one of Moses, who heard the cry of his people, who interceded with God on their behalf, and who addressed God's saving word to them. We will find both patterns as we turn to Israel's transition from tribal existence to a monarchy under Saul. The situation which we charted in Chapter One, regarding Israel's readiness for the monarchy, will serve as background for these prophetic stories.

Prophets and Institutional Change

A deep concern for the word of God penetrates the beginning of the books of Samuel. The first traces of prophetic concern emerge in 1 Samuel 1-3, the charming story of the prophet Samuel. Immediately we become observers of a complex familial situation where a man named Elkanah has two wives, Hannah and Peninnah. The former has borne no children "because the LORD had closed her womb" [1 Sam 1:5]. The storyteller does not bring us to their home in Ramathaim-zophim [1 Sam 1:1] to view the plight of her childlessness. Rather, he invites the audience to accompany this family on its yearly pilgrimage to the festival at the Israelite sanctuary in Shiloh. This drama occurs in a public setting, where worship and political ties are celebrated, and this fact should nudge us out of any cozy, familial interpretation of this inaugural story.

The life of Samuel will have profound political and religious implications for Israel. As a result, his birth, infancy, and childhood subtly point to the leadership role for which he will be carefully prepared. If any mother and father today take comfort from God's gracious answer to the prayer of their childlessness, they may also be challenged to reflect on the future of that child. Hannah's child was to be set aside for "the LORD all the days of his life" [1 Sam 1:11], involving him in the countless tangles of those who are called to provide leadership.

What specific conditions evoke the advent of prophetic leadership in Israel? In our section on the monarchy I discussed the political devastation experienced by the Israelites of the tribal confederation. The writers of Judges repeatedly summarized the problem as they saw it: "In those days there was no king in Israel; every man did what was right in his own eyes" [Judg 17:6]. The raucous events narrated in Judges 17-21 help to paint the picture of a society grimly proceeding toward chaos. In terms of biblical narrative, they demonstrate the pressing need for political change and leadership, and they pave the way for the prophetic speakers of God's word.

The disintegration of Israel's culture in these years also touched its religious institutions. In particular, the personnel who tended the sanctuary at Shiloh, a central place of gathering and worship, were affected. The opening chapters of 1 Samuel afford us a descriptive view of worship and its abuses at Shiloh, and the first prophetic oracle in the book directly concerns the downfall of Eli and his priestly sons, Hophni and Phinehas. Their abuse of the cult evokes a divine response just as clearly as does the petitionary prayer of Hannah. In turn, we will examine this prophetic utterance against Shiloh and then shift to the birth and call of Samuel himself.

The Man of God at Shiloh [1 Sam 2:27-36]

Eli, the priest who sat at the doorpost of the temple of God in Shiloh, had two sons whose priestly behavior merits no respect whatsoever. Hophni and Phinehas treated the "offering of the LORD" with contempt, because they would not content themselves with the portion allotted to them as priests—whatever a fork cast into the cauldron brought up should be given the priests [1 Sam 2:13-14]. In their greed they demanded portions of meat before it was cooked, so they could roast it with its tasty fat [1 Sam 2:15-16]. The narrator evaluates them severely: "thus the sin of the young men was very great in the sight of the LORD" [1 Sam 2:17a]. The greed of these ministers offended the LORD just as it interrupted the worship life of their neighbors.

Another aspect of their behavior vulgarized the sanctuary and scandalized the people. Eli's sons had sexual relations with the women who ministered at the door of the temple; this may imply sexual pressures exerted on the women by these priests [1 Sam 2:22-24]. They certainly offended the sensibilities of Israelite worshipers. Even when their father reproved them for their evil behavior they showed no inclination to heed his word and change their ways. The narrator suggests that their reproof had passed beyond human capabilities, so now God's intervention would be required.

These priestly abuses at Shiloh help to explain the need for divine intervention, a new order and a new era in pre-monarchic Israel. Do they also address us in our day? Where has greed infected the faithful exercise of ministry in our churches? Privilege blunts the clarity of worship and the directness of service to the people. Where do ministers take sexual advantage of their colleagues today? Ministers can exert subtle pressures on people, who in turn satisfy their emotional and psychic needs, as well as sexual desires. The question which Eli asks his sons provides a haunting query for today's ministers: "Why do you do such things? For I hear of your evil dealings from all the people" [1 Sam 2:23].

Then the storyteller provides a harbinger of future events: "Now the boy Samuel continued to grow both in stature and in favor with the LORD and with *people*" (my translation) [1 Sam 2:26]. This verse points to the reality behind these events, focusing both on the transition in leadership and on the judgment of the present order. In this text, disillusionment yields to hope for the future.

Finally a "man of God" (one of several terms for prophets) arrives on the scene. Although his identity remains concealed, his role seems clear. He will articulate God's word in this situation ("Thus the LORD has said" [1 Sam 2:27]). His oracle has a very simple structure. First, he reminds Eli that from the time of the Egyptian bondage his forebears in the tribe of Levi were chosen for ministry at the sanctuary. Second, the prophet condemns the priestly sons' behavior with a powerful rhetorical question: "Why then look with greedy eye at my sacrifices and my offerings . . . " [1 Sam 2:29]? This history of divine favor and accusation of greed could address countless situations, but the prophet's articulation pinpoints this word of God for this time and this place. Here is God's view of the present order.

There follows the divine sentence on this group of priests. Though God had once promised that Eli's family would minister in perpetuity, the future shall bring changes: "Behold, the days are coming when I will cut off your strength and the strength of your father's house, so that there will not be an old man in your house" [1 Sam 2:31]. God seemingly said to Eli: your dissolution as a priestly family has effected your demise, and the sign of this verdict will be the death of your sons, both on the same day [1 Sam 2:34]. What Eli was unable to rectify, God will now change—and Samuel stands at the very wings of the sanctuary, and of this story, waiting for his prophetic ministry to begin.

The decree of the man of God also introduces a promise, for God's activity never points solely toward destruction. A new priesthood shall emerge in Israel.

> *1 Samuel 2*
> [35] And I will raise up for myself a faithful priest, who shall do according to what is in my heart and in my mind; and I will build him a sure house and he shall go in and out before my anointed forever. [36] And every one who is left in your house shall come to implore him for a piece of silver or a loaf of bread and shall say, "Put me, I pray you, in one of the priest's places, that I may eat a morsel of bread."

Although the identity of this new "faithful priest" is not mentioned, the transfer of the ministry stands out clearly. A new order of priests shall replace the present group, one which will do God's will.

The man of God also points to one of the inevitable realities of prophetic history: God's transformation of a situation does not—indeed, cannot—occur internally. In our day, contrary to our hopes, the transformation of our churches and communities cannot always occur from within our traditional groups. In fact, we may find it necessary to listen to some very nontraditional prophetic voices in our midst—to the voices of those who are neither male, nor clerical, nor of religious communities, nor from the Western world.

Later, the books of Samuel and Kings do return to this oracle of doom, showing how it was fulfilled in the twisted events of Israel's history. In the very next incident, God tells the young Samuel what had been revealed in the word to Eli. When Samuel related it all to Eli, the old priest knew the word came from God, for it was the same word of doom which he had heard. Beyond this case, the death of Hophni and Phinehas comes to pass in 1 Sam 4:11, just as it was prophesied in 1 Sam 2:33. They both perished in battle at Ebenezer after the Philistine capture of the ark.

The narrator leads the audience through the agonizingly brutal details of the downfall of the house of Eli in 1 Samuel 4:1-22. Finally, Eli dies from shock over news of the capture of the ark and then Phinehas' wife goes into labor and bears a son just before her own death. The name she gives her son is Ichabod; literally, it means "there is no glory." The narrator explains that she named the child Ichabod, saying "The glory has departed from Israel" [1 Sam 4:21a]. His name aptly describes this shift in generations, this transfer of priestly ministry.

The oracle moves toward completion as various members of Eli's family meet their respective deaths. But not all of them died. Later in the David story, during his flight from Saul, he tricks Ahimelech the priest at Nob into giving him both a sword and bread for himself and his men [1 Sam 21]. When Saul's pursuit leads him through Nob, Doeg the Edomite reveals to the king that he had witnessed the priests aiding David [1 Sam 22:10]. When the enraged Saul orders the death of all these priests, he probably executes most of the descendants of the house of Eli. They had moved from Shiloh to Nob after the loss of the ark.

When Doeg, following Saul's order, slaughtered eighty-five of these priests, Abiathar was the only one who escaped. He became second chief priest for David. His preservation fulfilled the prophetic word, that one member of Eli's house would escape killing: he "shall be spared to weep out his eyes and grieve his heart" [1 Sam 2:33a]. Later, however, this word would more painfully work itself out during Solomon's reign. Since Abiathar had supported Adonijah, Solomon's rival for the throne, he expelled him "from being priest to the LORD, thus fulfilling the word of the LORD which he had spoken concerning the house of Eli in Shiloh" [1 Kgs 2:27]. The historian makes us well aware of the consequences of evildoing. Even more does he impress his hearers with the power of God's prophetic word: eventually it will come to fulfillment.

When a prophet proclaims God's word, it should instill both fear and hope. The people should fear because the oracle of doom will not be averted; they should hope because the restoration promised at its conclusion will not go unfulfilled. What the texts cannot calculate are the unsettling moments, days, even years when the hearers of the word await the achievement of God's inscrutable, inevitable word.

This opening oracle in the Book of Samuel introduces a new element into the realm of God's people. Certain chosen humans will, in the style of the messenger, relay God's word to Israel. But that word, while it invites a response of obedience and conversion from the people, achieves its own course. It will come about, whether Israel prepares itself or not. Finally, one might expect to hear this word specifically addressed to the political and religious institutions which affect the lives of all who appear in these stories. Prophets and prophetic words address the structures of our existence, rejecting some and establishing and legitimizing others.

God's Invitation to Samuel [1 Sam 3:1-4:1]

Hannah's promise to dedicate her son to God's service [1 Sam 1:11] has been fulfilled, and the young Samuel has already been "ministering to the LORD under Eli" for some time now [1 Sam 3:1a]. In spite of this family's dedication to God, however, the overall religious scene in Israel has deteriorated: "the word of the LORD was rare in those days; there was no frequent vision" [1 Sam 3:1b]. The influence of Eli's family still dominated, demonstrating the uncanny power of one family or group to affect the life and fate of a wide population. So these contrasting families do not present a tidy, intimate community for our observation; rather, they invite us to reflect on the possible social impact of any family. The oracle of the man of God [1 Sam 2] proclaimed divine judgment on Eli's house, and described its demise. This chapter begins by indicating the adverse impact of Eli's family on Israel's relationship with their God—communication of the word of God almost completely ceased.

The story of Samuel's call has long been a favorite story for those who are trying to discover who God would have them be. His is a story in which we can still participate, reflecting on the subtle words of God to us—so subtle that we may easily mistake God's call for another call. The adolescent Samuel returned three times to the aged priest whose voice he imagined he had heard. For those who treasure the notion of a personal call from God, the sense of having heard God's voice may become a treasured memory.

If one clings to a vocational memory like that, without ever flinching or questioning it, that person may not be able to hear a new word of God. In such a case, a certain deafness to God's word results from stubborn clinging to an older word of God.

Why can one speak of changing "words" of God? Precisely because it is so easy to fasten on Samuel's story when we try to confirm a call we had hoped to experience. When we possess certainty about the word we have heard, we are less prepared to hear new or surprising calls from God. A fresh reading of this story, then, may offer some clues for our own hearing of God's word. It must involve continual readiness to hear a word anew.

The word spoken by God often shatters expectations. Though Samuel expected to hear the voice of the elderly priest calling out during the night, he hears an unexpected voice, a voice whose speaker was slow to identify itself. Second, the voice addresses Samuel personally, so that a relationship between hearer and speaker would precede the content of the message. Third, the young man requires the assistance of another to perceive the source of the address. Fourth, the one who assisted Samuel to hear the word correctly was certainly no exemplary religious leader: he learned from an elderly priest, who could not direct even the ministry of his own sons. This first of the prophets received genuine guidance and direction from the spiritual head of a priestly line which would soon be bypassed by God, whose word would effect a transition of leadership in Israel. Finally, the young Samuel thrice reiterated his willingness to listen to the one who called him: "Here I am, for you called me" [1 Sam 3:5, 6, 8].

Several aspects of Samuel's experience challenge any easy hearing of God's word in our own lives. First, does the word I hear bear out my hopes, or does it surprise me and call me in new—and often undesirable—directions? The shattering of my expectations may provide a healthy criterion for judging the source of my audition. Then I also must ask if my hearing has simply framed a project for me, or has it shaped a relationship? Samuel responded personally to the divine speaker who called him by name three times, thus articulating his willingness to listen and to serve. Perhaps one criterion for judging that the word was from God is that it generally allows growth in relationship to precede concrete tasks.

The story presents Eli as Samuel's guide in the discernment of his experience. This crucial detail, in my opinion, suggests a need to entrust ourselves and the words we have heard to the confirmatory and testing discernment of another. For those who avail themselves of spiritual direction, young Samuel's trust in Eli may come as no surprise. Yet the biblical text challenges us precisely in this point. Eli provided neither a good model, nor had he been chosen by the young man. The elderly priest played his role primarily because of his priestly office at this sanctuary. Recall, this is the same priest who thought Hannah was inebriated because of her vocal prayer style. His ministry was marred by the greed and sexual excesses of his own sons' ministry. By all accounts, Eli was an unlikely guide!

This peculiar story presents us with an anomaly. One who does not hear well and act on the word of God in his own life still may help another to hear the divine call with clarity. Perhaps the narrator suggests for us an unlikely model of ministry. Even when the interpreter seems flawed, one who is willing to listen attentively and to respond generously stands a chance of hearing God authentically. The willingness to enter into relationship emerges as a more important factor than a perfectly crafted ministry-style.

After Eli helps Samuel to identify the speaker who called his name, God sends an oracle of doom to the young man. It is expressed in words which basically repeat the prophecy of the man of God from Shiloh against the house of Eli [1 Sam 2:27-36]. This version of the judgment on Eli's family specifies the old priest's sin: "for the iniquity which he knew, because his sons were blaspheming God, and he did not restrain them" [1 Sam 3:13]. His avoidance of the offenses committed by his sons had such a lethal impact that "the iniquity of Eli's house shall not be expiated by sacrifice or offering for ever" [1 Sam 3:14]. Samuel's dream-vision condemns the very man who had helped him to recognize God's call and to answer to it. Is there any wonder that he "was afraid to tell the vision to Eli" [1 Sam 3:15]? Who finds it easy to relate God's message? Only when one has a message of prosperity does it seem easy to prophesy.

God's word effects wonders, even at the tainted sanctuary in Shiloh. At Eli's courageous insistence, Samuel communicates to him everything which he had heard and seen; he withholds nothing of the terrible message. Eli's courage is transformed into a serene resignation when he hears of the doom to come upon him, especially when he recognizes its source: "It is the LORD; let him do what seems good to him" [1 Sam 3:18]. It seems that the word of God offered to Eli the possibility of accepting his doom with dignity and with faith in the LORD. Could we stand with such dignity as we watch God's word pierce so cleanly through our own flawed histories? Eli offers some hope to all who are unable to control the actions of their families, friends, and colleagues. One can still help others to hear the word of God with integrity, then to hear even a difficult word oneself, and still live with composure and fidelity. Eli's portrait may offer us more latitude for imitation than many of the other characters in these narratives.

This first section of the Samuel narratives concludes with a powerful theological reflection.

> *1 Samuel 3*
> [19] And Samuel grew, and the LORD was with him and let none of his words fall to the ground. [20] And all Israel from Dan to Beer-sheba knew that Samuel was established as a prophet of the LORD. [21] And the LORD appeared again at Shiloh, for the LORD revealed himself to Samuel at Shiloh by the word of the LORD. [4:1a] And the word of Samuel came to all Israel.

Samuel's word and the LORD's word both stand forth in this appraisal of the young prophet. The LORD's word constituted God's means of revelation to Samuel, assuring his recognition as a prophet by "all Israel." Moreover, the LORD did not let young Samuel's words fall fruitless. His words share in that most important characteristic of God's word: they accomplish what they proclaim.

Eli must have remembered the oracles of doom which Samuel uttered against his house when his sons perished in battle and the ark was captured at Ebenezer [1 Sam 4:1-22]. The word of God actualized itself. Ironically, Eli's own death followed his chagrin over the loss of the ark. So his tragic death represents the demise not only of Eli's family, but also of the ark as a mode of discerning God's presence. No longer can Israel trust that God goes wherever the ark goes.

The ark effectively yields to the word of God as symbol of divine presence. Vision gives way to hearing as the way to discern divine presence and invoke God's protection. The loss of the ark and this death point to a far more pervasive transformation of life, society, and religion within Israel. Eli stands on the far side of this division, a figure serenely composed yet shrouded in tragedy.

Prophets and the People

The cycle of stories about Elijah provides for us a dramatic view of prophetic life and activity [1 Kgs 17-19, 21; 2 Kgs 1-2]. Famous stories about Elijah the prophet feed our own imaginations just as they did for some ancient writers. Elijah and the widow, Elijah on Mount Carmel, Elijah and the "still small voice"—these stories form the legacy of a powerful mediator of the word of God. From the social and historical perspective of ninth-century BCE Israel, these narratives presuppose a time of economic growth and security, especially for those who comprise the royal and landed circles. Friendly relations with neighboring countries typify the era, symbolized by the marriage of Ahab to Jezebel. Such alliances imply both religious and economic commerce, and the obligation to preserve faith in the God of Israel will be sorely tested. The contest with Baal at Carmel typifies the problem.

The Elijah stories in 1 Kings come from an era much earlier than the deuteronomic writers and preachers. They probably come from groups who found the prophets to be the primary mediators of God's word and will for them. These prophetic circles also viewed their prophets as the most important voices to be heard in the political scene in Israel. Following up on the crucial roles played by Moses and Samuel, these writers told stories in which the prophet Elijah really directed affairs in the northern realm. The graphic stories invite us to stand with prophets like Elijah in their passion for the well-being of all the people, united in worship of their one God.

These prophetic legends emphasize the marvelous acts of power effected through the prophetic activity. Through such deeds, God encourages this people to stand firm in time of need. This image of Moses as the miraculous savior of the people Israel looms over the figure of Elijah in these stories. A connection between Elijah and Moses seems logical, since groups in the northern kingdom of Israel cherished the Moses traditions more than the court scribes in Jerusalem. As in the northern traditions, the covenant which Moses mediated will form an important religious horizon for Elijah and his followers.

Three stories in 1 Kings 17 introduce the cycle of stories about the prophet Elijah. First, he proclaims a drought to Ahab [1 Kgs 17:1] and then flees for safety east of the Jordan river [1 Kgs 17:2-7]. Then Elijah meets a widow in Zarephath, who offers food to him from the food God provided for her and her son [1 Kgs 17:8-16]. Then the prophet resuscitates the widow's son, after his sickness resulted in death [1 Kgs 17:17-24].

Each of these stories would interest Israelites in the later eras. The LORD's control over the forces of nature effected the drought, which threatened to impoverish Ahab and his circle, but also wreaked havoc on the growing peasant population. The narrators subtly interweave the royal concern in stories which spell out the negative impact of Ahab's rule over the entire socio-economic spectrum. All suffer from the drought, including the prophet himself, who must flee to the region east of the Jordan. There he must remain submissive to the word of the LORD [1 Kgs 17:2, 5] and depend on divine nourishment delivered by ravens. An Israelite audience could hardly fail to connect their situation with memories of their ancestors' journey through the desert. Led by Moses, they depended on divine assistance for food and direction.

Each of Elijah's travels in this chapter are dictated by the word of the LORD: to the brook Cherith [1 Kgs 17:3] and to Zarephath of Sidon [1 Kgs 17:8-9]. The widow experiences God's graciousness when faced with her son's starvation. A powerful word of God provides bread and oil for the one who trusts, just as God fed the Hebrews who cried out in their desert wanderings. Moreover, through God's word this woman's son is brought back to life, just as the Egyptian generation's offspring had come alive again in the land of promise. God's new saving acts ring true to ancient graces.

Elijah's speech in these two incidents replicates two modes of prophetic speech—the oracle and the prophetic prayer. In the first story (provision of meal and oil for the widow) the prophet delivers a typical, self-consciously prophetic oracle.

1 Kings 17
[14] Thus says the LORD, the God of Israel, "The jar of meal shall not be spent, and the cruse of oil shall not fail, until the day that the LORD sends rain upon the earth."

The second narrative describes the new life to the widow's son. In it Elijah "cried to the LORD" repeatedly [1 Kgs 17:20, 21], a stance hardly surprising to those who remembered Moses' prayers to God for his people. The power of God's word in the oracle exhibits itself in almost immediate fulfillment, while the outcry of the prophetic leader evokes a response from God.

The raising of the widow's son personalizes the life-preserving stance of Elijah. This prophet, whose ministry has already provided food for the starving, now attends more profound life issues. The divine word acting through him can even return the dead to life. Moreover, the narrator uses a word which adds to the wonder of it all: "the LORD harkened to the voice of Elijah" [1 Kgs 17:22]. When God calls to the people and commands them to do something, this same word "harken" denotes obedience to God. Here, God seems to obey the outcry of the prophet, who articulates the plea of the oppressed. When we are a bit chilled by the pattern of events in our world, such a word may begin to rekindle hope that the LORD does hear the cry of the poor.

Other aspects of the Elijah narratives in 1 Kings 17 suggest a Moses-like perspective for the ministry of Elijah. The drought he proclaimed could dredge up memories of the plagues in Egypt; as in the ninth century, the ultimate goal in Egypt was to engender knowledge of the LORD as God. This drought concludes in 1 Kings 18, where the LORD receives recognition as the god who controls nature as well as history. Those who stood on Mount Carmel saw the vanity of Baal worship and came to know the LORD better.

The identity of those who suffer in the drought suggests another perspective on this story. The first story of the drought's effect features a widow from a foreign country. If Ahab and Jezebel's religious policies were the real reasons for this ninth-century drought, why does the storyteller focus first on a Sidonian widow and not the harm done to the royal household? Does the widow's fate simply provide a more concrete and evocative situation for the hearers of the story? I suspect that care of widows, fatherless, and aliens guided the prophetic writers; accordingly, this story deals with representatives of each of these categories.

Perhaps the prophetic storytellers imply that the harm done to the monarchy would not suffice for an outcry to the LORD. Rather, the crying out which does attract God's attention is that of the protected groups in Israel, symbolized in this story by a widow from Zarephath and her fatherless son. Their fate results from the royal leadership in Israel, its religious syncretism, and the socio-economic stratification brought about by Canaanite commerce under Ahab and Jezebel. It seems ironic that the first victim of the drought brought on by Ahab and Jezebel's policies should be a woman from Jezebel's home people. This marriage of political convenience ultimately bodes ill even for her own people! This story suggests that God hears the cry of the suffering of all peoples who suffer. The prophetic circles do not invite narrow ethno-centrism.

For us, the widow's trust in the word of a God whom she knew not stands as powerful challenge. Could we connect her trust with her experience of desperation over the impending death by starvation of her only child? This narrative implicitly links genuine trust in God's word with situations of deprivation. Do her situation and her response

184 The Prophets As Speakers of God's Word

match ours in any real fashion? Desperation does seem to render people more available and attentive to the prophetic word of God.

Finally, Elijah's outreach to a Phoenician woman challenges us to extend our concern to all. Since we are unable to respond to every oppressed person or group which comes to our attention, we make concrete choices each time we engage in prophetic ministry for any group. Elijah's concern for the foreign woman calls on us to broaden our horizons. Do we discover certain ones which we generally exclude because of personal or ideological bias? These prophetic stories challenge us to eradicate any parochialism in our prophetic concern. We might recall Jesus'own rejection in Nazareth, after he recalled Elijah's concern for this widow [cf. Lk 4:24-26]. Elijah's attention to this woman should evoke no less from us than it did from Jesus. Elijah's stance also suggests good reason for prophetic concern with Israel's leadership, the kings.

Prophets and Kings in Israel

Prophecy in Israel basically coexisted with the monarchy. Although prophetic figures stand out in Israel's earlier history, such as Abraham, Moses, Miriam, and Deborah, their appearances are scattered and do not seem connected to each other. Certainly there were prophets during and after the Babylonian Exile, but this religious group or phenomenon experienced its heyday during the time of the kings. One reason for this coexistence seems to be the prophets' role in the designation of kings.[9] In similar fashion, none but a prophet endowed with the word of God possessed the authority to condemn or reject a monarch whose behavior did not live up to the standard set for kings. In this section we will examine some stories of royal designation and rejection by prophets. Naturally, these narratives suggest ways of relating to contemporary leaders, and the spiritual vision needed for such activity.

Samuel and Saul [1 Samuel 9-10, 15]

As part of the transition from the chaos of the era of the Judges, God directed Samuel to designate Saul as prince over the people [1 Sam 9:15-18]. Samuel takes Saul up to the roof of a house where they had been at a banquet. Samuel then tells Saul to dismiss his servant; this was to insure privacy. Then the prophet proclaims to him "the word of God" [1 Sam 9:27], and anoints Saul with oil. Then he explained the ritual.

> *1 Samuel 10*
> [1] Has not the LORD anointed you to be prince [*nagid*] over his people Israel? And you shall reign over the people of the LORD and you will save them from the hand of their enemies round about...

Then Samuel lists three "signs" by which Saul could recognize God's presence [1 Sam 10:1b-8], and all of "these

[9]Studies by Antony Campbell have drawn my attention to texts in which prophets and kings are so closely related. A summary of his research and theology of these prophetic stories will appear in his work, *Enjoying the Old Testament* (Wilmington, DE: Glazier, forthcoming). I am grateful for the opportunity to review his text and to learn from it.

signs came to pass that day" [1 Sam 10:9]. The word of God has powerfully accomplished that which it proclaimed: three signs come to fulfillment. More importantly, Saul does become prince by power of the word and the gesture of anointing.

This designation of a new leader is not due to some divine whim. Israel's storytellers have made clear the desperate need for new leadership: the Philistine menace. According to the story, God had promised Samuel that Saul would "save my people from the hand of the Philistines; for I have seen the affliction of my people, because their cry has come to me" [1 Sam 9:16b]. The complaint of God's people has always resulted in divine action, just as in Egypt. Israel virtually cries out to God in 1 Samuel 1-3, so God's response should surprise no one. But the precise answer of God taps a totally new resource. In 1 Samuel 9-10, Samuel mediates God's designated leader for Israel; the permanence of the prince/king ushers in a style of leadership quite different from the Judges. Israel's experience of chaos and oppression opens them to a new word of God, one by which God constitutes a new reality and offers a new hope.

Saul's leadership, however, never lived up to the great expectations placed on him. Soon we find that his divine authority has been removed. In 1 Samuel 15, God directs Saul to punish the Amalekites who had brutalized the Hebrew tribes on their journey from Egypt. Saul only partially destroys the enemy after defeating them; he spares their king Agag, as well as his choicest flocks. He does not fully carry out God's order not to spare anything of Amalek's [1 Sam 15:3].

It is difficult not to experience some empathy for Saul,

who has obeyed the basic thrust of the command
at the complete destruction of the enemy. Even if he acted
on pragmatic grounds when he preserved the best of the
booty, the material needs of his people surely have motivated
him. Such care for his people deserves some praise. So his
rejection by the LORD comes as a genuine surprise, until we
hear its reason. Saul failed to comply fully with God's
directives, the "word of the LORD."

How does the prophet participate in this story? Samuel's
role now requires him to criticize the king's arrogation of
authority to himself. Saul should not develop a royal
consciousness, in which the progress and security of the state
are his prime concerns. Then his responsibility for his actions
would rest solely on his own decisions and his popularity
with the people. Samuel establishes God's word as the final
criterion of royal behavior: "Because you have rejected the
word of the LORD, he has also rejected you from being
king" [1 Sam 15:23b]. God's word should rule the king's
behavior just as it directs the prophet's ministry to the
people. Samuel's role in both the designation and rejection of
Saul points ultimately not to his own power but towards
obedience to the word of the LORD as the ultimate criterion
of effective leadership.

Obedience to God's word is never easy, and particularly
in cases like that faced by Saul—destruction of the enemy—
it often seems ludicrous. For us today, Samuel's charge to
Saul may seem almost a case of blind, unthinking obedience,
something we should be loathe to imitate. Is there no scope
for human judgment, for calculation of benefits, for norms of
morality? To us Saul seems caught in a web of contradictions
which render him a truly tragic figure. Even Samuel may

have struggled with this command. When he received the word of the LORD to reject Saul, Samuel "was angry, and he cried to the LORD all night" [1 Sam 15:10-11]. His subsequent obedience to God's word demonstrates only that Samuel submits to a word which he experienced as coming from God. Such a word can evoke pathos on his part, misunderstanding on the part of all. In desperate straits, however, the inscrutable word of God commands adherence.

Precisely at times like this one, the prophetic voice will do battle with the voice of wisdom in our midst. How can we moderate the calculations of the wise with the fragile ability to hear God's word? Such is our challenge today, not only in world affairs, but even with our churches. How do we hear the word of God honestly, without the tampering of our own machinations? These storytellers, who trusted the prophetic word, could not avoid the dilemma between human reflection and divine word within their own times. Neither can we bypass this tension in our lives. Perhaps the tragically clear message of this narrative proved as great a problem in Israel's day as in our times. This confident spirituality of trust in God's word may reach us in a slightly relativized form. Since it coexists with competing spiritualities in our canon (e.g. wisdom), the inspired biblical writers do not seem to give it absolute sway.

Elijah and Ahab [1 Kgs 21:17-24]

Elijah's rejection of Ahab proves far less disturbing than Samuel's action toward Saul. Ahab's wife, a Phoenician woman named Jezebel, has been viewed according to two traditions: in one, she was daughter of a king; in the other a daughter of a priest of Baal. Israel's historians depict Ahab's reign as a time infected with attempts at absolute monarchy and worship of Canaanite deities. These abuses suffice to evoke a prophetic message from God to Ahab.

His crime against Naboth (illegal acquisition of his vineyard through false accusation; we will return to this story in Chapter Six) seems to justify the severity of his condemnation. Ahab's exercise of power resembles the acquisitive, royal mind of Solomon far more than the responsible leadership of David. Where Nathan's parable about the poor man with his ewe was able to move David to repentance [1 Samuel 12], Ahab crassly executes the peasant who refused to barter his inheritance from the LORD. Ahab's penitential gestures and dejection [1 Kgs 21:27] hardly match the outright confession of David. Ahab's confession proved sufficient to avert the prophetic word uttered against him: "because he has humbled himself before me, I will not bring the evil in his days; but in his son's day I will bring the evil upon his house" [1 Kgs 21:29]. The curse passed on to his descendants.

The prophet's role in this story invites our reflection. Ahab's condemnation and rejection comes not as the result of a judicial proceeding based on Israel's Torah; that would be an impossible scenario in view of the monarch's power. Rather, the prophet delivers the word of the LORD, which actualizes both the judgment and the curses of the covenant. God's word breaks in through a prophet when the social and political situation renders such intervention practically unimaginable. The word of God again functions to criticize and to provide new life and power for people who are powerless to effect change in the royal sphere. Just as their

Hebrew forebears experienced oppression and servitude by
the whim of the Pharaohs in Egypt, Naboth's fate represents
a new occurrence of such injustice. Even without an explicit
outcry for justice, the speaking God responds to the cry for
liberation of the entire people. Later, a new vision of
leadership will occur when Elisha arranges to have Jehu
designated as the head of a new ruling family.

For us, Elijah's encounter with Ahab provides a moment
of hope. It suggests that situations of seeming hopelessness
are not necessarily so, that the outcry of the oppressed
renders God partial to those who suffer. If we find ourselves
in Naboth's situation—facing physical death, or death by
exclusion and silencing—there is yet a thread to hold on to:
the word of God addresses the unwarranted suffering of an
individual or a community. The pathos raised by suffering
evokes a word from God—words of rejection which call
forth something new.

Elisha and Jehu [2 Kings 9]

The curse against Ahab's house achieves its goal when
Jehu replaces Jehoram as king in Israel. In a scene reminiscent
of Saul's designation by Samuel, a young prophet sent by
Elisha specifies Jehu as king. In a private act of anointing, the
young prophet clarifies Jehu's role ("I anoint you king over
the people of the LORD" [2 Kgs 9:6] and his mission ("you
shall strike down the house of Ahab your master, that I may
avenge on Jezebel the blood of my servants the prophets, and
the blood of all the servants of the LORD" [2 Kgs 9:7]). This
audacious action of the young prophet leads Jehu to even
more daring feats. He rebels against Jehoram and kills him in

battle, and finally kills Ahaziah. The chilling beginning of Jehu's bloody reform stands justified in the story because it accomplishes Elijah's curse of Ahab. The LORD had sent this oracle against Ahab: "As surely as I saw yesterday the blood of Naboth and the blood of his sons—says the LORD—I will requite you on this plot of ground" [2 Kgs 9:26]. By focusing the destructiveness of God's word on the crime against Naboth, the prophet also prepares for a fresh mode of viewing reality. A monarch must heed the just claims of individuals like Naboth.

This curse and its destructive power tend to alienate us as contemporary hearers of the word of the LORD. Yet we may take some encouragement from its message that crimes against the poor evoke divine anger and response. Moreover, the power of God's word to bring about what it proclaims can steady wavering hearts, especially of those who complain of suffering and injustice in their midst. When our lament lacks the depth and the staying power to continue the outcry, the prophetic word of the LORD addresses the concerns of those who lack strength to speak.

Conclusion

The word of God mediated through prophetic figures stands ready for evaluation, just as did the monarchy and the temple as institutions which channel human and divine interaction. One of the strengths of a spirituality focused on the prophetic word of God resides in its ability to strengthen all who suffer, especially those who lack strength and courage to voice aloud their complaint. It also plays a role in transforming and reforming institutions, if the prophetic figures accept their full responsibility. The prophetic designation of Jehu concretizes in a particular way the realizing power of the word of God. There it completes the rejection of Ahab's unjust and idolatrous rule by introducing a new ruling line in Israel. This kind of word does not simply moralize about suffering and offer hope in an afterlife. Rather it proclaims the contemporary truth boldly and gradually effects a changed reality and vision.

No spiritual focus is without its weaknesses, and the spirituality of the word of God also has its problem points. A most glaring problem besets those who feel that they hear the word with utter clarity: discernment loses its role, and the wisdom of those gifted from within may go unheard and unattended. I reflect not only on some examples of fundamentalist preaching in our day, but also on those for whom certainty of the word provides complete closure on issues. Bluntly put, word of God spirituality ought not overshadow the presence of the divine in every other spirituality, especially wisdom spirituality. The next chapter will present a homiletic spirituality of the word of God. Perhaps Israel's biblical preachers will provide avenues for further reflection on this unsettling question.

IN THE SHADOW
OF MOSES AND LEVI:
HOMILETIC SPIRITUALITY
OF THE WORD OF GOD

Early prophetic stories and legends directed our attention to quite specific incidents in Israel's history. There we found the word of God addressed to a concrete situation of social deterioration, to the particular needs of individuals, and to key leaders in Israel. In turn, those stories highlighted certain prophetic persons in Israel, inviting the audience to marvel at their boldness as well as their power for effecting change.

In the previous chapter I asserted that prophetic spirituality was characterized both by content and by its mode of communication. Prophets self-consciously articulated God's word for particular situations of widespread, public interest. The narratives presented in Chapter Five show the prophetic word of God as a self-conscious act on the part of the speaker. Normally oracular formulas, such as "thus says the LORD" or "the word of the LORD" witness to the prophet's sense of authority. The audacity to speak out boldly certainly required some kind of internal assurance that the prophetic word derived from God. That need explains their use of the formulas.

Internal certainty, however, rarely suffices by itself to embolden a prophetic voice. External criteria and assurances also encourage and prepare the speaker. Often such external assurance comes from an important role model. In the deuteronomic view of Israel's history, Moses stands as the premier prophet, so the characteristics of his prophetic role furnish a resource for the Deuteronomists when they retell stories of later prophets.

Prophetic voices were notably few after the return from Exile in Babylon. The Chronicler certainly realized this void, and if he were writing a disinterested history he easily could have included all the prophetic stories for memory's sake. But the books of 1-2 Chronicles present a history for life, that is, a program for present living based on the lessons of history. In his retelling of Israel's history, the phenomenon of prophecy was too important for him to bypass. He would transfer the speaking of the word of God to people and institutions of his era. In the Chronicler and the Deuteronomists we will discover how Israel's preachers imagined the word of God and exhorted Israel to listen carefully for even a whisper of the divine.

Deuteronomic Spirituality of the Word of God

Our study of the deuteronomic vision of God's prophetic word will lead us to ask how they used older traditions and beliefs in order to develop their own theology and spirituality. In this section, we will observe the effects of viewing prophets through the prism of Moses' roles. In particular, these preachers will emphasize two of Moses' achievements as models for prophetic activity: mediator for the people and Torah-giver.

MOSES AND PROPHETIC MEDIATORS

Studies of Israelite prophecy rarely begin with Moses. Nor has my discussion of prophetic spirituality in Chapter Five started with him. But when we attend to the prophetic oracles, actions, and narratives in the historical books we cannot neglect Moses, the speaker of God's word in the days of Israel's origins. Moreover, the deuteronomic preachers viewed all of Israel's story through the lens created by Moses' farewell address to Israel in the book of Deuteronomy. Books like Samuel and Kings witness to Israel's living out of Moses' covenant in Deuteronomy, so later prophetic saviors and speakers of God's word stand in the shadow of his limelight.

In this section we will observe two levels of tradition about Moses as a prophet. First, some suggestions of his role as a prophet come from the early narratives about Moses in Egypt and in the desert wanderings. These references stand beside notions of Moses as a military and political leader of a revolutionary new community. Second, the deuteronomic portrait of Moses, especially in the Book of Deuteronomy, makes him appear more like a prophet than the earlier stories would have suggested. These different notions of Moses seem to describe a developing idea of his importance in Israel; at the same time, they suggest the growth of a spirituality of the prophet.

Moses in Exodus and Numbers

The earlier narrative traditions in the books of Exodus and Numbers showed some inkling of Moses as a prophetic figure. In Pharaoh's court he brought God's word about the Hebrews, that they should be allowed to go apart for worship. Repeatedly we hear that one purpose of God in the plagues Moses introduced was that the "Egyptians shall know that I am the LORD" [Exod 7:5]. After Moses led the Exodus from Egypt, he and the Hebrews migrated to Sinai, where he experienced God on the holy mountain. God commands Moses to relay the divine word to the people Israel in a scene reminiscent of prophetic messages: "And Moses went up to God, and the LORD called to him out of the mountain, saying, 'Thus you shall say to the house of Jacob, and tell the people of Israel'" [Exod 19:3]. Later, during the desert wanderings, when Moses complained of the burdens of leadership, God commanded him to take aside seventy elders; God would impart to them some of the spirit of Moses so they could share his burden [Num 11:10-23]. After Moses' "spirit rested upon them, they prophesied" [Num 11:25]. Evidently Moses possessed a spirit of prophecy, and this insight provided food for thought by the Deuteronomists.

Moses in Deuteronomy

The opening line of the Book of Deuteronomy portrays it as a speech of Moses to Israel. It opens with these words: "These are the words that Moses spoke to all Israel beyond the Jordan in the wilderness . . . " [Deut 1:1]. As Moses reminds Israel of God's love for them during all these years, his speech begins to sound like a farewell address. He exhorts the people to live up to the covenant with God which they had entered into, and a long section of the book contains the code of conduct which this relationship with God requires of them [Deut 12-26]. Moses sounds like a preacher all through the book, and it is this tone which suggests that deuteronomic spirituality is homiletic. After all the sermonizing, the book ends on a surprising note.

> *Deuteronomy 34*
> [10] And there has not arisen a prophet since in Israel like Moses, whom the LORD knew face to face, [11] none like him for all the signs and the wonders which the LORD sent him to do in the land of Egypt, to Pharaoh and to all his servants and to all his land, [12] and for all the mighty power and all the great and terrible deeds which Moses wrought in the sight of all Israel.

Suddenly this preacher of God's covenant has become a prophet, and every prophet in Israel must measure up to Moses.

The Deuteronomists must have contemplated Moses' life and words for a long time. Perhaps they compared him with other great speakers of God's word whom they remembered. Teachers and preachers who had ancestral roots in northern Israel might recall stories about Elijah and Elisha. Since northerners had no great regard for the Davidic kings in the south, and did not worship in Jerusalem, their affection and esteem for Moses could have grown very easily. As they grew in their devotion to Moses and his teaching as their greatest leader, they could describe him in terms familiar from their own prophetic legends. Because Moses was their greatest religious spokesperson, he would gradually take on the qualities of every other religious leader who came after him. Eventually, Moses became their premier prophet.

This prophetic portrait of Moses allows its artists to gather together details of his life, as the stories describe him. At a most fundamental level, Moses communicates God's word of saving response to the Hebrews in Egypt. First of all, he mediates God's word to Israel, as does every prophet. That word is a saving word, which contains two distinct ways of addressing people. First, it poses a critical challenge to those social structures which alienate and oppress God's people. Second, it energizes the people by promising a new type of life together. In other terms, the prophet issues oracles of doom and of salvation. Speaking God's saving word also leads to the prophet's mediating activity—invoking God's compassion on the people. This kind of prophet, then, must be a person of passionate concern poured out in prayer to God. Deuteronomic preachers could easily call upon Moses as the example *par excellence* of impassioned concern for those in need.

This prophetic portrait of Moses, however, does not emerge from self-conscious rhetoric on his own part. Rather, the Deuteronomists have portrayed him in prophetic garb. Moses does not mediate God's word as consciously in his own role as do the prophets in the books of Samuel and Kings. The crucial point for the Deuteronomists, however, is that the source of the word or statement is considered to be God, who has spoken to us humans. In this viewpoint the clarity or appropriateness of an oracle do not constitute it authentically prophetic; rather the divine source of the word marks it as prophetic. Here lies its real authority for the life experience of its hearers.

Word of God in the Moses stories, then, emerges as a word that saves, energizes, and creates. The personal activity and mediation of prophetic figures always concretizes the human experience of God. The deuteronomic preachers understood Moses in this way, so whenever Israel later experienced desperation they concluded that chosen persons would arise and speak like Moses. They would transmit words of challenge and re-creation, like Moses' words, which would accomplish what they proclaimed. In the deuteronomic books prophets critique the people who resort to other gods; they have relapsed into "Egyptianism," a code word for the social and religious life-style of any oppressive culture. They also speak words which promise something new, a life in the covenant relationship of mutual dignity and responsibility. The deuteronomic word of God, then, recalls a God who saves people from chaos and oppression, whose word recreates life with a new vision.

The reason I described the deuteronomic view of Moses as a prophet was to grasp better deuteronomic experience and expectations of prophecy. If the Deuteronomists had Moses on their imaginative horizon when they narrated legends about later prophets, then the various aspects of his life and leadership also enrich their description of other prophets. This way of telling stories about religious heroes and models has become part of the spiritual heritage from which most of us draw. We often paint ancient heroes in larger-than-life strokes, hoping that their example can lead to imitation on our part. At other times, we tend to judge contemporaries by comparing them to ancient personages, and those whom we choose for our models indicate our visions of ourselves.

The Deuteronomists chose Moses as their criterion for

judging who truly spoke the word of God in their day. The choice of Moses as model for later prophets implicitly indicates a neglect of other ways to discern God's will, such as divination, casting of lots, or debates among the intelligentsia. This deuteronomic choice finds God speaking through a leader who leads people to freedom, who engages them in a covenant with God, and who carefully reports to them God's desires for the entire fabric of their lives. Such sensitivity to God's word and passion for God's people could prove to be the marks of our own listening to God's word and proclamation of it to others. These qualities may describe the contours of prophetic ministry today.

Moses and Elijah [1 Kings 19]

The deuteronomic preachers seem to have Moses in the back of their minds as they retell stories of the early prophets in Israel. In Chapter Five we looked to the Elijah stories as examples of prophetic concern for all human life. There we found that his concern for the oppressed of his day seemed nurtured by memories of Moses and his concern for the oppressed Hebrews in Egypt. Now we will look for other features of Moses' portrait which appear in the stories about Elijah. There we will find more elements of a spirituality of prophetic concern for our day.

Elijah's ability to stop the rains in northern Palestine places him in a similar category with Moses and Aaron, during the Egyptian plagues. Elijah's provision of food for the widow and restoration of life for her son provide new signs and wonders for all Israel. In this his ministry resembles that of Moses. The stories of Moses' liberating activity at the sea do not use prophetic language, but a prophetic role should not be denied on such grounds. Like Elijah, who responded to the critical needs of his day, Moses' actions in Egypt form part of God's response to the Hebrews who "cried out for help and the cry under bondage came up to God" [Exod 2:23].

Elijah's triumph over the Baal prophets of Mount Carmel is narrated in 1 Kings 18. The victory of the LORD has a double conclusion. Elijah creates a bloodbath as he slaughters the Baal prophets [1 Kgs 18:40]. Then God graciously concludes the devastation of the drought when a small cloud comes into view and showers the land with rain [1 Kgs 18:41-45a]. When Ahab told Jezebel all that Elijah had done, he complained about the slaughter of their Baal prophets and neglected the marvelous return to fertility which the rains promised. She reacts in accord with her own religious convictions: she determines to slay this prophet, who challenged her way of life and worship [1 Kgs 19:1-2].

Elijah's flight into the desert leads him eventually to Mount Horeb, where Moses himself had fled after killing the apostates in his company [Exod 33:17-34:9; 1 Kgs 19:3-8]. At Horeb many of Elijah's experiences parallel those of Moses. Both approach a cave on the mountain, so that Elijah came to the very place where Moses had experienced God [1 Kgs 19:9-14 and Exod 33:21-23]. In each story, the leader experiences some ambiguous indicators of divine presence— natural elements of storm, wind, earthquake,and lightning. Both learned, however, that the LORD's reality was not to be found in the storm, but only to be heard [for Moses cf. Exod 19:16-25]. The narrator describes Elijah's experience of God.

1 Kings 19

[11] And he said, "Go forth, and stand upon the mount before the LORD." And behold, the LORD passed by, and a great and strong wind rent the mountains, and broke in pieces the rocks before the LORD, but the LORD was not in the wind; and after the wind an earthquake; [12] and after the earthquake a fire, but the LORD was not in the fire; and after the fire a still small voice. [13] And when Elijah heard it, he wrapped his face in his mantle and went out . . .

The prophet heard the LORD. His Canaanite neighbors, by contrast, experienced Baal in storm phenomena. Israel should find God differently than did the neighboring peoples.

In slightly different language, the "still small voice" suggests the importance of hearing the word of the LORD for those who would proclaim that word today. The core of prophetic witness, then, resides closer to the discerning and contemplating of God's word than to the planning and execution and speaking of the program to others. Listening for God's word should characterize not only the preacher and the teacher, but those who imagine themselves engaged in prophetic ministry of any kind. The story of Elijah, like that of Moses, reminds us again of the marriage of attentive listening and passionate concern which can bring new vision and fresh life to the world.

The description of Elijah's prophetic ministry contributed to the portrait of the prophet Moses, but it also receives much from the Moses traditions. Many in Israel could find direction and courage in the lives of Moses and Elijah, speakers of God's word for freedom and for communal life centered on God. For the exilic generation these stories offered a powerful vision of the prophetic word which had the power to nudge the disheartened from their despair. Today, in similar fashion, many people magnify the personalities of modern day prophets like Martin Luther King, Jr. and Archbishop Desmond Tutu. Each of them has drawn deeply from the spirituality of Moses, and has spoken God's word courageously as they share their visions and spiritualities. They are not the only ones called to such spirituality in our day; we, too, are called.

PROPHETS AND TORAH

Moses had a strong connection with Israel's law, which we call Torah. When the writers of Deuteronomy included a huge law-code in the middle of Moses' sermon, they remained faithful to the story in Exodus 19-24. There the ancient narrators recalled God's appearance to Moses, followed by the Decalogue [Exodus 20] and the Law of the Covenant for Israel [Exodus 21-23]. The priests had also envisioned all the laws and regulations for Israel as God's transmission to Moses at Sinai. Moses as Torah-giver was a notion developed from Israel's ancient traditions.

Here the focus does not rest so surely on saving acts of God as on the words of Torah which issue forth at Horeb, words which will constitute this community. Moses as prophet coexists with Moses as lawgiver to his people, for the Deuteronomists imagined him transmitting the Torah of the LORD: for God said "Stand here by me, and I will tell you the commandment and the statutes and the ordinances which you shall teach them ... " [Deut 5:31]. Moses' prophetic ministry also involved transmission of Torah to the people. His role extends even to the structuring of life in the community through transmission and repetition of Torah.

In deuteronomic spirituality, the prophet also takes responsibility for the Torah by which the people shall live. Moses as law-giver will find his progeny reminding kings and people of the sense and the stipulations of Torah, and of the grave consequences of rejection of this teaching. By the time these preachers have completed their retelling of Israel's history they have also demonstrated that prophets provide the key to all significant aspects of Israel's life together. Moses, and his followers act as liberators of the people, speakers of words of salvation and condemnation, mediators for the people, and transmitters and teachers of Torah.

The care for Torah characterizes the description of several prophets like Moses. We shall focus only on three passages, but each of them demonstrates the prophetic connection with Torah. Elijah confronted Ahab and condemned him because of his oppression and execution of Naboth. Next, the prophetess Huldah takes on the role of authenticating Torah during the era of King Josiah. Finally, the sermonic explanation for the destruction of Samaria provides a third instance of Torah joined with prophets.

Naboth's Vineyard [1 Kings 21]

In Chapter Five we discussed the story of Naboth's vineyard as an example of the prophet's power to reject a king. Here we examine the basis of his condemnation, the royal neglect of Torah. This story recalls the theft of a peasant's vineyard by the king and queen of Israel, Ahab and Jezebel. Naboth's vineyard lay next to Ahab's palace, and the monarch determined to secure it for a convenient vegetable garden. But Naboth had a different view of the land; it was not a commodity which could be traded or sold but was "the inheritance" of his forebears [1 Kgs 21:3; cf. Deut 19:14]. He realizes that he cannot sell it. Ahab's perplexity shows that he realizes that he cannot purchase the land. His only hope to acquire it derives from Jezebel's alternative view of the royal role. From her Phoenician viewpoint, monarchic rule does not have a covenantal relationship with the people and the land; it is only an institution by which one can rule or manipulate. She taunts her husband by asking: "Do you now govern (literally, "do kingship") in Israel?" [1 Kgs 21:7]. In her view, he is not a king unless he assumes absolute power.

This story also provides an example of the impersonal processes of institutional bureaucracy. Jezebel sends directives or letters to deal with their opponent; a letter renders personal contact unnecessary. Perhaps we are reminded of another king who sent letters: David sent written directions to have Uriah killed. Even more startlingly, Jezebel uses Torah for her own, unjust goals: she arranges the false accusation of Naboth by twisting the law of Exod 22:28: "You shall not revile God, nor curse a ruler of your people." The whole crafty plan works so smoothly that Ahab secures the land without arousing any public outcry or legal redress.

Elijah's activity begins when the "word of the LORD" directs him to meet Ahab. He is to confront the ruler with his crimes, and to pronounce God's sentence against him [1 Kgs 21:17-19]. His prophetic role leads him to challenge the royal couple's crass way of ignoring traditional Israelite values and to show how they usurp legal processes for their own ends. His charge reveals the royal desecration of Torah:

"Have you killed, and also taken possession?" [1 Kgs 21:19]
Then he shall issue God's sentence against Ahab: "Thus says
the LORD: 'In the place where dogs licked up the blood of
Naboth shall dogs lick your own blood'" [1 Kgs 21:19]. The
prophet applies Torah to this crime.

This story shows a prophet proclaiming and applying
Torah when royalty attempt to live above God's law. The
story and curse we have just read probably come from early
Elijah legends, but the Deuteronomists added some verses
when they retold the story. The most important additions
are the following:

> *1 Kings 21*
> [21] Behold, I will bring evil upon you; I will utterly sweep
> you away, and will cut off from Ahab every male, bond or free,
> in Israel.
> [23] And of Jezebel the LORD also said, "The dogs shall eat
> Jezebel within the bounds of Jezreel."
> [24] Any one belonging to Ahab who dies in the city the dogs
> shall eat; and any one of his who dies in the open country the
> birds of the air shall eat.

Deuteronomic writers were not satisfied with the curse
aimed at King Ahab; they also added a curse for Jezebel [v.
23]. Then they condemned the entire following of Ahab
with the curse for "any one belonging to Ahab" [v. 24].
They realized that all those involved with the wicked
monarchs deserved condemnation. They apply a touch of
realism for their contemporaries: all those who side with the
monarch participate in an evil monarchy. Here the
deuteronomic preachers show the prophet Elijah delivering
God's word about the monarchy.

Our contemporary prophetic challenge in public life

retains many of these core values. What responsibility have we to see that laws are not twisted to benefit privileged groups? Law should serve all those whose liberty and dignity are endangered. In face of powerful opposition (usually of commercial nature) how do we help people to protect their God-given inheritance? It might concern the land of Native American groups or the customs, traditions, or languages of other minorities. Prophetic ministry may extend as far as the tedious legal work required to bring abuses of Affirmative Action policies to appropriate judicial bodies. Prophetic vocation may call for continual writing of personal and persuasive letters calling for more just application of the law. Activities like these may be as prophetic as public demonstrations and protests. Elijah's intervention in favor of Torah calls us to many and varied responsibilities.

Huldah the Prophetess [2 Kgs 22:14-20]

In the seventh century BCE King Josiah ordered repair work done in the Jerusalem temple. During the course of the project, a scroll of the Torah was found in one of the storerooms. Hilkiah the high priest exclaimed: "I have found the book of the *Torah* [translation mine] in the house of the LORD" [2 Kgs 22:8]. He then had it read to the king. Josiah was moved to repentance by the severity of divine judgment which he heard in the scroll. Then he sent Hilkiah and other officials to consult Huldah the prophetess, "inquire of the LORD . . . concerning the words of this book that has been found" [2 Kgs 22:13]. He wanted to learn if the book of Torah which been discovered during the temple repairs was actually authentic.

Josiah was motivated by fear: if all he had heard was true, then Israel's infidelity was so great that it would bring on the covenantal curses. Some have marveled that they asked a woman. The narrator tells about their trip to consult her so naturally that no surprise about the woman prophet seems intended.

Huldah responds with an oracle which subtly confirms the authority of the Torah. She describes the equivocal outcome of their history of abusing the covenant: on the one hand, God's wrath will not be quenched, but Josiah shall die peacefully because of his repentance [2 Kgs 22:16-20]. She need not proclaim anything about this document found in the temple since she articulates its meaning. She says: "Thus says the LORD, Behold I will bring evil upon this place and upon its inhabitants, all the words of the book which the king of Judah has read" [2 Kgs 22:16]. In other words, the book of Torah does reveal God's intentions for Israel. She reveals that Torah does contain the word of God for king and people.

Many people think that this book of the law is roughly equivalent to the book of Deuteronomy. Huldah's prophetic role leads her to authenticate the Torah document, and she secures its role in this community. Huldah's particular prophetic ministry draws her to exhort king and people to adhere to Torah. She resembles other prophets, like Moses, who also mediate Torah.

Preaching on the Fall of Samaria [2 Kgs 17:7-23]

We now turn to the fall of Samaria and the deuteronomic sermon which reflects on this tragedy [2 Kgs 17:7-23]. Our text comes from writers in Jerusalem who viewed the destruction of Samaria and the deportation of the ten northern tribes as just punishment for their many sins. In their view, the military strength of the Assyrians was not the reason for Samaria's downfall. It occurred because "Israel had sinned . . . and had feared other gods and walked in the customs of the nations" [2 Kgs 17:7-8a]. The writers carefully list all the forbidden worship practices they can recall; avoiding idolatry becomes the essence of the commandments and the covenant given to Israel.

False worship has become a central focus of the prophetic preaching to Israel. In the prophetic view, this ravaged country could have avoided destruction had it harkened to God's prophets.

> 2 Kings 17
> [13] Yet the LORD warned Israel and Judah by every prophet and every seer, saying, "Turn from your evil ways and keep my commandments and my statutes, in accordance with all the law [torah] which I commanded your fathers, and which I sent to you by my servants the prophets."

The prophets of Israel almost seem to be an institution, rather than individuals. So we may wish to know how the deuteronomic preachers define "the prophets."

These prophets communicated Torah to the monarch and to the people. The writers of Deuteronomy described their role, saying that God would put God's word in the mouths of the prophets [Deut 18:18]. Since the sermon in 2 Kings 17 connects Torah with the prophets, we may assume that the preacher sees prophetic speech as word of God, including Torah. Then Deuteronomy warns those who do not heed

God's word of Torah, for God will requite them [Deut 18:19]. So prophets as a group now have the duty of proclaiming God's law for Israel.

The conclusions reached about Samaria match perfectly the program established in Deuteronomy. Since the prophets had proclaimed the Torah to Israel, who had not obeyed, their present fate simply concretized the curse. Once again the prophetic role seems to derive from the portrait of Moses, for in the very next chapter the preacher again attributes the Assyrian conquest to Israel's disobedience. That text, however, reasons differently: "because they did not obey the voice of the LORD their God but transgressed his covenant, even all that Moses the servant of the LORD commanded" [2 Kgs 18:12]. So we observe these preachers viewing the prophets in the image of Moses; part of their role is to transmit Torah and exhort Israel to obey its commandments. The prophets— like the Deuteronomists themselves!—have become preachers in the book of Kings.

The relationship of Torah and prophecy suggests important issues for our own spirituality. We might ask: what does it mean to derive Torah from the prophets? Our biblical traditions link Torah to Moses, but why was he portrayed as the model prophet? I suspect that they focused attention on the prophetic word because its source was divine speaking, and fulfillment of God's word was amply demonstrated in these books. The fulfillment of a prophetic word builds trust in other prophetic words, and this trust could motivate Israel to obey Torah.

These theologians provided motives for covenant fidelity, and offered hope for the faithful. Constant attentiveness to God's word provides a spirituality for times of distress and confusion. In our experience the description of the Scriptures as word of God helps to confirm for us the possibility of hearing God by attentive listening to the word of God in the Scriptures. In times of crisis and doubt we develop trust and gain hope that what we hear is not simply the reflection of our own voice or thoughts.

Absolute trust in the prophetic word also entails dangers. Such a spirituality may encourage one to transfer authority from the challenge of concrete situation to the word as it has been articulated in the past. For example, prophetic oracles were originally addressed to specific situations: to assume that they can easily address a contemporary problem is to make more of God's word than the prophet intended. When an ancient word too easily displaces fresh reflection and listening for the word of God, the prophet's word is idolized. Unless we can listen to hear God speaking in new and unaccustomed ways, as these prophets did, we risk not hearing the prophetic word which God would speak to us now. A spirituality which relies solely on perceptions gained in the past does not grow, nor can it remain adequate to life's process and paths. The prophetic word invites us to listen always, to expect the unexpected.

Chronicler's Spirituality of the Word of God

When we search for the word of God in 1-2 Chronicles a very different notion greets us. After contemplating the prophets in Samuel and Kings, some of the variations will surprise us. The person who seemed to crystallize the prophet's role in the book of Kings was Elijah; those books devote six chapters to his life and ministry [1 Kgs 17-19, 21; 2 Kgs 1-2]. Second Chronicles gives Elijah only a single appearance, but let us reflect on it now.

The Chronicler discusses the wickedness of King Jehoram of Judah, who reigned from 849-842 BCE. The author accuses him of constructing high places and leading the people of Judah astray [2 Chr 21:11]. Then a letter came from the prophet Elijah. It read as follows.

2 Chronicles 21

[12b] Thus says the LORD, the God of David your father, "Because you have not walked in the ways of Jehoshaphat your father, or in the ways of Asa king of Judah, [13] but have walked in the ways of the kings of Israel, and have led Judah and the inhabitants of Jerusalem into unfaithfulness, as the house of Ahab led Israel into unfaithfulness, and also you have killed your brothers, of your father's house, who were better than yourself; [14] behold, the LORD will bring a great plague on your people, your children, your wives, and all your possessions, [15] and you yourself will have a severe sickness with a disease of your bowels, until your bowels come out because of the disease, day by day."

Elijah condemns this king because he has led Judah into idolatry just as Ahab had done to Israel. The Chronicler's theology of sin and punishment resembles deuteronomic preaching. They had set two ways before Israel, life or death; they could choose the way to either, by obedience or disobedience. In this view, we can easily account for the evil we suffer: it is the result of our sin. Here we find the sternness of the deuteronomic Elijah, but he lacks the human passion of those stories.

Elijah's letter places responsibility for all the people's ill on the sins of the monarch. Jehoram's people shall suffer as much as Ahab caused Israel to suffer. What stands out for our reflection is not the condemnation, but the great responsibility placed on the king's shoulders. Both the Deuteronomists and the Chronicler recognized the deteriorating effect of sinful leaders on a society. In contemporary terms, some speak of a "structural sin" embedded in society. Its continued existence is assured unless some person or group takes drastic steps to eradicate those patterns of action. Elijah's letter to Jehoram reminds all leaders, not just those in governments, of the awesome task which lies at hand for them. Since the issue he took with Jehoram concerned worship, religious leaders can also hear his challenge.

If Elijah's message seems familiar, everything else about the incident seems unexpected. Elijah has not written letters in the books of Kings, nor has he mediated God's word to the kings of Judah. Of course, we must recall that 1-2 Chronicles presents only the history of the kings of Judah. The Chronicler judged the northern kingdom severely, and focused exclusive attention on Jerusalem and the temple. For these reasons, he need not retell the northern stories in which Elijah confronts Ahab.

The Chronicler had new ideas about the prophetic word of God in his own day. Although 1-2 Chronicles do not omit the prophets of old, this preacher fastens on the vibrant activity in the oracles, liturgical music, and preaching of the Levites of his own day. Here he finds the prophetic spirit active among Jews after the return from Exile. When ancient prophets are missing, the word of God still comes through the Levites. The spiritual vision they present closely resembles the covenant-centered spirituality of the Deuteronomists, updated for their times. With these resources, the Chronicler's Jewish audience could hope and expect to hear God's word for their lives, just as their ancestors had during the time of the monarchy.

A Levitical Prophet [2 Chr 20:13-17]

The next example of prophetic speaking comes during the reign of King Jehoshaphat of Judah (873-849 BCE). The kings of Ammon and Moab threatened battle against the king in Judah. Like a true monarch in Israel, the king calls a ceremony of national fasting and lamentation to beg God's help. In a moving prayer of lament, the king himself stands in the temple and cries out to God for help [2 Chr 20:5-12]. His prayer reminds us of many psalms of lament in the book of Psalms: it includes his complaints, his petition to the LORD, and confesses his trust.

Then something strange happens, which we almost never find in the psalms which are like his prayer: someone delivers God's response. The word of God addresses all the inhabitants of Judah and Jerusalem, as well as the king: "Fear not, and be not dismayed at this great multitude; for the battle is not yours but God's" [2 Chr 20:15b]. Here the word of God comforts the people.

The speaker of God's word also concerns us here. We are not listening to the words of a temple priest, nor of a famous prophet. Let us attend to the Chronicler's introduction.

> 2 Chronicles 20
> [13] Meanwhile all the men of Judah stood before the LORD, with their little ones, their wives, and their children. [14] And the Spirit of the LORD came upon Jahaziel the son of

> Zechariah, son of Benaiah, son of Jeiel, son of Mattaniah, a
> Levite of the sons of Asaph in the midst of the assembly.

Only if we have learned to listen carefully to the Chronicler's
genealogies do we discern the speaker's identity: he is a
Levite of the family of Asaph. We might recall the
importance of Levitical genealogies when we discussed the
personnel whom David appointed for the temple. Here the
same careful listing occurs, and we discover a Levite speaking
with the spirit of the LORD.

Even though the Chronicler tries hard to give more
respect to the Levites of his day, they do not stand on a par
with the priests. So why does a Levite utter this oracle of
God's word? It seems that Levites took their temple ministry
very seriously, and many of them taught the Torah during
the centuries after the Exile. They would have known Torah
better than their priestly colleagues, so they could easily
compose prayers and sermons which fit the particular
occasion. As in our day, some of those who study the word
more diligently actually speak God's word more authentically,
even when they lack ecclesiastical status.

Prophets and Music [2 Chr 29:25-30]

This curious connection of liturgical music and the
prophetic word occurs in the story of King Hezekiah's
cleansing of the Jerusalem temple [2 Chr 29]. After giving
the regulations for sacrifices, the Chronicler describes the
musicians.

> 2 Chronicles 29
> [25] And he stationed the Levites in the house of the LORD
> with cymbals, harps, and lyres, according to the commandment

of David and of Gad the king's seer and of Nathan the
prophet; for the commandment was from the LORD through
his prophets.

[30] And Hezekiah the king and the princes commanded the
Levites to sing praise to the LORD with the words of David
and of Asaph the seer. And they sang praises with gladness,
and they bowed down and worshiped.

While we might not connect prophets and liturgical hymnody
together, the Chronicler does. First, God had ordered this
particular choral arrangement through the prophets [2 Chr
29:25]. Second, some of the hymns of praise used the words
of Asaph the Levite seer, who stands on a par with David in
this verse.

Those who expect a solitary prophet to proclaim an oracle
of doom against injustice will hardly recognize this strange
mediator of God's word. The liturgical chorister, however,
may account for the stirring of God's word within the hearts
of many worshipers. Perhaps the Chronicler recognizes the
possibility that the spirit of such hymns was the spirit of the
LORD. Since many people have suggested that the prophets
chanted their oracles, we may trust the Chronicler's vision a
bit more. If we feel cautious about mixing ministries of
liturgical praise and prophetic address, we probably will not
sit comfortably with the Chronicler's vision here. The
weakness of such an arrangement is the tendency to
telescope all ministries in a few people. Yet we might recall
that Levites did not hold positions of highest status. And if
we can take the Chronicler's view at face value, we might
also find profound encouragement and spiritual vision for
those who compose and provide music for the liturgical
assembly.

A *Levitical Sermon* [2 *Chr* 15:1-7]

Again we meet a Levite who clearly experiences the spirit of the LORD before speaking out. This Levite also shares the prophetic spirit, and he encourages the reigning king to continue his faithful following of the LORD.

> *2 Chronicles 15*
> [1] The Spirit of God came upon Azariah the son of Oded, [2] and he went out to meet Asa, and said to him, "Hear me, Asa, and all Judah and Benjamin: The LORD is with you, while you are with him. If you seek him, he will be found by you, but if you forsake him, he will forsake you. [3] For a long time Israel was without the true God, and without a teaching priest, and without law; [4] but when in their distress they turned to the LORD, the God of Israel, and sought him, he was found by them . . .
> [7] But you, take courage! Do not let your hands be weak, for your work shall be rewarded."

This is one of the shortest of these sermons in the books of Chronicles. It demonstrates a type of preaching which we might expect from this homilist of renown who composed the book. The preacher explains their past experience to them: they were long separated from God. But when they cried out to the LORD—in a prayer stance dating back as far as the Hebrew outcry in Egypt—God heard them and found them. The message here is not one of warning, but of encouragement to stand fast in the paths of faith and fidelity.

If this prophetic word leaves us a bit deflated, I suggest that we are victims of our prejudices about prophets. Not all prophecy emphasizes social critique, particularly in times like the Chronicler's, when the Jews do not fully control their own society. But God's word does address them in language of adhering to God through worship and obedience to the covenant. In a situation of oppression, fidelity to worship might indeed prove to be a daring political stance. But that matters less than their willingness to assert their identity as people chosen and saved by God. Should they not listen to God's word for the present day, even if it simply encourages their present paths?

Preachers might take some comfort from this Levite's sermon. How many preachers wish their sermons were as inspired as this Levite's! Even those who interpret the Scriptures, as he seems to do, might do so in the prophetic spirit. Perhaps even the biblical interpreter can hope for a share in God's spirit!

In these brief examples of prophetic activity in 1-2 Chronicles we find surprising ways for the word of God to reach the worshiping community. The proclamation of a liturgical oracle of hope for Jehoshaphat came from the mouth of a Levite prophet. The music and singing of the worshiping assembly were decreed by a word of God; with attentive listening and singing, participants may expect to hear a word of God when they worship together. Finally, the preacher's homily may be a graced occasion for the word of God to express encouragement as well as warning. These indications of the spirit of prophecy active in Israel's worship at the temple seem to complement the Chronicler's concern to legitimate, console, and include many worship officials by his construction of genealogies.

Perhaps the Chronicler urges us to search hard for the word of God addressing us in liturgical worship. We are not advised to assume its presence there, but this spirituality gives the benefit of the doubt to those who minister to God in the holy temple. At the least, the Chronicler challenges us to hope for more than we expect.

Conclusion

A Mosaic vision informs the entire book of Deuteronomy, which in turns textures the historical books of Joshua through 2 Kings. In a particular way, then, this pattern of the oppressed crying out to the LORD and the prophetic response of liberation by God underlies the meaning of prophecy. Prophets exist for the freeing of those in bondage, for their guidance into a new life. In the pattern of Moses they also assume the responsibility of challenging their people to live according to the Torah. A deuteronomic spirituality of the word of God reminds us that prophetic ministry entails critique of society and religion, but it also reveals a new and alternative vision for life. The Torah stands as God's program for Israel's new life. We might ask what elements form our own prophetic reality.

The Chronicler presents a view of Israel's relationship to God which seems quite similar to that of the Deuteronomists. It focuses on obedience to God's law, which lies at the heart of the covenant. But the social situation of his Jewish audience differed greatly from that of the Deuteronomists' audience. In his day there were no kings for prophets to address, so the word of God has now to be heard in the only place where Jews can gather, in the temple. This preacher feels that certain liturgical actions are prophetic, even when the mediators may not be totally aware of God's spirit at the time. Perhaps this preacher knows from experience that the realization of prophetic experience sometimes comes only in hindsight. Might that be possible for us? The Chronicler calls us to careful discernment about our own lives. We should look not only to the future when we imagine a prophetic role; we may have exercised such a ministry in the past, even though unknowingly.

FROM BIBLICAL STORY TO LIFE: BIBLICAL SPIRITUALITY AND OUR SPIRITUALITY

One reason that families pass on stories of their forebears is to keep good stories alive. We cherish narrative memories because they so enrich our sense of identity. Stories of our ancestors describe the world from which we have come, and the view which we learn in a story may set boundaries for our future. As we come to know better who we are, we can learn to choose what we will do in a particular situation, or who we will be in the future.

For the Jewish and Christian faith tradition, the books of Samuel, Kings, and Chronicles provide a storehouse of narrated memories to ponder and retell. In the three parts of this book we have listened anew to stories from early days of the monarchic times in Israel. Some of them come to us from the Jerusalem court. Many of these bear marks of "state truth," which casts the actions and policies of the ruler in the best possible light. We read optimistic stories of David's rise to power, mostly from 1 Samuel. There we found him portrayed as a liberator of the tribes of Israel; he saved them

.. chaotic times of political unrest and violence under the Judges. Sobering stories of David's court and personal life surprise us in a document that began so enthusiastically; they remind us that the king's responsibilities to the people have just begun when the consolidation of power in Jerusalem is achieved. These stories describe the possibilities and the dangers involved in royal leadership in Israel. For us, narratives implicitly paint a landscape of the routes to follow and pitfalls to avoid if we wish to serve people in their everyday lives. These stories might catch the attention of people whose work could be seen as government service.

Other stories can be traced to archives of the Jerusalem temple. Solomon's construction of the house of God in the early years of his reign stands in glorious relief in 1 Kings 6-8. Temple sources, however, have given us only a small part of the stories in these books; much of the temple lore that informs our knowledge of the temple actually comes from other texts left by temple officials. We find these in the priestly traditions of the Pentateuch, and many more in the Psalms. Since there is much about the temple which these books do not say, what they do affirm stands out the more clearly. Beautiful natural resources can be fashioned by human imagination and intelligence to give honor to the Creator of all. Of course, these records tread a fine line between seeing the temple as God's house, or as a place for Israel to meet God. For us, these stories raise questions about our understanding of the fine churches, shrines, and religious art which we create and appreciate. Do they enshrine and confine God? Or do they lead us to God? Such reflections might challenge church people to reexamine their goals and ministerial procedures.

Many stories in these books originated in circles of prophets and their disciples. Several of these narratives implicitly suggest that prophets really had charge of Israel's life, since they designated and sometimes deposed kings. They could certainly challenge the monarchy. Sometimes we are surprised that prophetic legends stand alongside stories from the court, which imply that God accompanied David and ultimately brought him to power in Israel. Other prophetic stories emphasize the prophet as savior when Israel cried out in distress. That role extends to particular situations of need and also to generational shifts. As a response to the distress of Judges 17-21, prophets played a constructive role in the shift from tribal government to monarchy. The stories dramatize the prophet's experience of God's word for particular times and places. For us, they implicitly challenge us to listen for fresh words from God about the social and religious settings in which we live. They also hint at the courage we may need to develop in order to articulate those words from God. These notions challenge all those who feel called to some type of prophetic ministry and life-style.

These stories, as we have seen, prove one of the best ways of passing on spiritual values in an implicit fashion. This artistic sharing of religious and social values through narrative art can be described as a narrative spirituality. Of course, such spirituality is not confined to the biblical text. We began our inquiry by reflecting on family stories and on a legend about two saints. Narrative spirituality is what we often discern and cherish from reading biographies of great people, from hearing stories about marvelous leaders and very holy people. It is what we pass on when we retell as accurately as possible a story which another told us.

Narrative spirituality can imply another activity, one which we have not yet discussed. When we attempt to describe our own spiritual journey and values to another we often begin by telling stories about our experience. We hope that our friend, or companion, or pastor, or director will be able to discern our spirituality from what we narrate to them. This sharing of sacred story often happens when people share their faith together, either formally or informally. It characterizes one distinct approach to spiritual direction. There the director stands with another, helping to discern from his or her story the spiritual vision and invitation offered by God.

Some of the biblical stories we have heard together may cause you to say "ah, yes, I understand *that*" or "that line really woke me up." When that moment comes, then we begin to receive spirituality from biblical story. At the same time we grow in our ability to describe our own spirituality.

The process of telling our stories—either as individuals or as groups—adds a further element to the process. Stories derive from human experiences, and narration provides the first level of interpretation of life's activities. When we examined the biblical stories in these chapters, we did not ask; "What was the original experience behind the story?" We did not focus on that question, since biblical historians ask it. When we discuss our own lives, however, it will be difficult to ignore the prior experience: that was where we had to choose what to do and how to live. Our own developing spiritualities, then, might consist of a variety of experiences, narrations, and subsequent interpretations of them.

Very often storytellers add comments or emphases to the

story; sometimes they cite the opinions of others, at other times their own. We found commentary in Gregory's preaching insertion into the story about Scholastica. We recognized it there because we have experienced this phenomenon before. Perhaps our parents or teachers retold stories from the Bible or from history. Interpretation of stories offers us an excellent way of passing values from one generation to the next. When these life values involve faith in God, I propose to speak of them as a homiletic spirituality.

In the books of Samuel and Kings we found clear evidence of interpretation of early stories. We could no longer distinguish contributions from the court, temple, or prophetic circles as easily as we had in the narratives. We began to notice an overlay of remarks which judged the monarchy and the Jerusalem temple by a new criterion—their adherence to the covenant and Torah of Moses. They charged the royalty with responsibility for much of the social and political upheaval they were experiencing; the sins of the kings brought on Israel's troubles.

Furthermore, they implied that the sin had become almost hereditary. Where they speak of "Jeroboam's sin" or "Manasseh's sin", we might speak of structural or institutional sin. In our day, many analysts ascribe much of the trouble in our world and society to the particular values and social/ economic policies of current world powers. Critique of both Marxist and capitalist systems gives an example of the search for contemporary "structural sin." Some prophetic voices in our midst call for a reorientation of our values, with greater emphasis on spiritual vision and justice. It is not surprising that those who experience oppression would retell biblical stories differently than do our leaders. The homiletic spirituality of the Deuteronomists addressed Israel's leadership with as challenging a message as certain prophetic groups articulate in our day. We find in these texts resources for a new vision of society and church in this century.

The Chronicler's history also draws attention to Israel's monarchy, the prophetic voice, and the Jerusalem temple. Since this writing addressed Jews who had no king in Judah, they began to think of David in terms of worship. Here his reputation as founder of the Psalter makes much sense. Although this "historian" does not chronicle the past with the accuracy which we imagine to be "historical", he fulfills an important role. The Chronicler shows fifth-century Jews how to live: they should attend to the temple—where they do have independence from the colonialist power of Persia. He directs Jews to transfer the enthusiasm of David's military and bureaucratic disciples to the present. They might think of David's contemporary followers in terms of temple priests and ministers—who did minister in the Chronicler's time. Worship and obedience to the covenant might bring greater stability and peace to Judah. Such a homiletic spirituality comes from the Chronicler's interpretation of Israel's history. In our day, we often observe much greater emphasis on religious involvement in those countries where religion is least tolerated. There we might search for a full-scale homiletic spirituality in their retelling of old stories.

Our journey through these books has followed a two-dimensional path of inquiry. We ask about the life situation of the tellers of the stories, and hope that we will discover there a spirituality of both leaders and disciples in each life setting. Narratives offer vital information about the situations which motivate people, but they usually are implicit in the story. The second path invites us to travel through time, reflecting on the fresh interpretations in the preaching of the Deuteronomists and the Chronicler. There we learned how our ancestors themselves interpreted the biblical story and retold it to fashion a new spirituality for their day. We might discover there the roots of much of our own conversation, writing, speaking, and preaching.

The variety of spiritualities which we encounter in these books almost astounds us. We learn that no single concept— whether it be something so important as "covenant" or "steadfast love"—can adequately describe the spirituality contained in them. The reality is far more complex, and requires much more of us as interpreters, just as it demanded far more of those who heard these stories and preached them many centuries ago. The various narrative and homiletic spiritualities of these books teach us how spiritual families and movements and visions change, adapting their faith to new life situations. The changes may take place over time, as we find in the deuteronomic preaching; or they may occur as people move from one life-situation to another. For us, this variety of options should not lead to confusion or depression, fearing that we have no spirituality to grasp. We are called to discern our own deepest motives, beliefs, and choices, culled from our own stories. When we have done this, we can speak of our narrative spirituality. We are also invited to reflect on our ways of retelling the old stories of our lives and faith: there we shall discern our own homiletic spirituality.

Finally, we might compare the spiritualities we have discovered in these books with various Christian spiritualities. Biblical spiritualities may resemble the great spiritual traditions in western Christianity—the different ways of living faith in the several Christian churches. In the Roman Catholic church the inspiration of numerous religious communities witnesses to modern variety of outlook and historical situation. The Franciscans, Dominicans, Jesuits, Carmelites, and many others hark back to a time when a founder's experience was narrated to others, who shared the story and passed it on. Each of these groups has had to interpret the experience of the founder, by formulating constitutions for their life together. Like the Deuteronomists and the Chronicler, later generations have tried to reinterpret the pristine experience for new situations. Few of these groups have completely passed out of existence even though each remains admittedly incomplete. None of them fully expresses the meaning of the Christian call to life in the spirit. From our viewpoint, each of these spiritualities continues to cry out for later Christians to "complete me".

What could it mean to "complete" a spirituality? Simply that this perception of mine is authentic, but not a perfect articulation of life in God's spirit. So, each of these spiritualities cries out for further attention, to those matters and issues which they substantially neglect. This collection of successive and various spiritualities in the books of Samuel, Kings, and Chronicles cries out for us to complete them. It is a reassuring call, for we also hear that there remains room for each of us, as peculiar and as special as we are.

FOR FURTHER READING

Here I list some works which proved quite helpful in my reflection on the Books of Samuel, Kings, and Chronicles. Although I also consulted other works of a more technical nature, these offer the most promise for those pursuing a spirituality of these books.

Commentaries

Conroy, Charles. *1-2 Samuel, 1-2 Kings.* Old Testament Message #6. Wilmington, Delaware. Glazier. 1983.

Mangan, Celine. *1-2 Chronicles, Ezra, Nehemiah.* Old Testament Message #13. Wilmington, Delaware. Glazier. 1982.

Brueggemann, Walter. *1 Kings.* Knox Preaching Guides. Atlanta. John Knox. 1982.

Other Works

Brueggemann, Walter. *David's Truth in Israel's Imagination and Memory.* Philadelphia. Fortress. 1985.

Campbell, Antony. *Enjoying the Old Testament.* Wilmington, Delaware. Glazier. [forthcoming]

Heym, Stefan. *The King David Report.* London. Abacus; Sphere Books, Ltd. 1984.

Petersen, David L. "Portraits of David." *Interpretation* 40:2 (1986) 130-142.

APPENDICES

APPENDIX I

ERA OF THE MONARCHY IN ISRAEL

1020-922 The United Kingdom or Monarchy
        1020-1000 Saul [Samuel: prophet]
        1000-961 David [Nathan: prophet]
        961-922 Solomon

922-722 The Divided Monarchy to the fall of Israel (North)

Israel's monarchs	*Judah's monarchs*
Jeroboam (922-901)	Rehoboam (922-915)
	Abijam (915-913)
	Asa (913-873)
Nadab (901-900)	
Baasha (900-877)	
Elah (876)	
Zimri (876)	
Omri (876-869)	
	Jehoshaphat (873-849)
Ahab (869-850) [Elijah: prophet]	
Ahaziah (850-849)	
Jehoram (849-842)	Jehoram (849-842)

Jehu (842-815)   [Elisha: prophet]   Ahaziah (842)
                                                   Athaliah (842-837)
                                                   Jehoash (837-800)
Jehoahaz (815-801)
Jehoash (801-786)

                                                   Amaziah (800-783)
Jeroboam II (786-746)

                                                   Uzziah (783-742)
Zechariah (746)
Shallum (745)
Menahem (745-738)

                                                   Jotham (742-735)
Pekahiah (738)
Pekah (737-732)

                                                   Ahaz (735-715)
Hoshea (732-721)

722 **Fall of Samaria**

722-587   The Decline and Fall of Judah (South)
                                        Hezekiah (715-687)
                                        Manasseh (687-642)
                                        Amon (642-640)
                    [Huldah: prophetess]   Josiah (640-609)
                                        Jehoahaz (609)
                                        Jehoiakim (609-598)
                                        Jehoiachin (598)
                                        Zedekiah (597-587)

587   Fall of Jerusalem
587–538   Exilic Period
538   Decree of Cyrus; return to Zion/Jerusalem

APPENDIX II

LITERARY DEVELOPMENT OF SAMUEL, KINGS, AND CHRONICLES*

In this chart I offer a schema for the development of these books during the monarchic era in Israel (1020-587) and the Exile (587-538). Historical periods appear in the same fashion as in Appendix I, but here we focus on the biblical books rather than on the important persons and dates. In the left column are the biblical texts which concern the history of a particular period; in the right column appear those sections of these books which probably were composed and written during an era. In our use of this chart we must recall that the dating in the right column is approximate at best, and oftentimes disputed.

(1020-922) *The United Kingdom*

"Story" of the given period	*Passages "composed" in period*
1-2 Samuel	Story of the Ark (1 Sam 4-6; 2 Sam 6)
1 Kings 1-11	Story of Saul's Rise (1 Sam 9-14)

*Format adapted from Douglas Knight.

235

1 Chronicles 10-29   Story of David's Rise
                                      (1 Sam 16:14–
                                          2 Sam 5:9)
2 Chronicles 1-9   David's Court History
                                      (2 Sam 9-20; 1 Kgs 1-2)
                                      Court annals, temple rec-
                                      ords (begun in this era)

(922-722) The Divided Monarchy to the Fall of Israel (North)

1 Kgs 12–2 Kgs 17   History of Solomon's
                                      Kingship (1 Kgs 3-11)
2 Chronicles 10-28   Prophetic Stories: Elijah
                                      and Elisha (1 Kgs 17–
                                      2 Kgs 9)

(722-587) The Decline and Fall of Judah (South)

2 Kings 18-25   Deuteronomic Code
                                      (Deut 12-26)
2 Chronicles 29-36   Deuteronomic History #1
                                      (first version of Deuter-
                                      onomy—2 Kings)

(587-538) The Exilic Period

                                      Deuteronomic History
                                      #2 (final version of
                                      Deut–2 Kings)

(538-333) The Persian Period

                                      1-2 Chronicles

APPENDIX III

THE DEUTERONOMIC HISTORY*

Deuteronomy	I PREAMBLE: Moses presents the law of the LORD for life in the land
Joshua—2 Kings	II HISTORY of Israel's life in the land, with a special reference to this law
Joshua	A *Under Joshua:* an account of Israel's conquest of Canaan
Judges 2:7-10	B *Reflection:* transition of generations
Judges—2 Kings	C *Life in the Land:* a history continues
Judg 2:11—1 Sam 7	1 *Under the Judges*
Judg 2:11—9:57	a up to Abimelech
Judg 10:1—1 Sam 7	b after Abimelech

*Structure of Deuteronomic History adapted from Antony Campbell

1 Samuel 8-12	2 *Reflection:* transition of institutions
1 Sam 13—2 Kgs 25	3 *Under the Kings*
1 Sam 13—1 Kgs 8	a up to temple construction
1 Sam 13—2 Sam 6	1) to coming of Ark
2 Sam 7—1 Kgs 8	2) after coming of Ark
1 Kgs 9—2 Kgs 25	b after temple construction
1 Kgs 9—2 Kgs 17	1) to fall of the North
2 Kgs 18-25	2) to fall of the South

THE CHRONICLER'S HISTORY

1 Chronicles 1-9	The world before Israel's Monarchy (lists)
1 Chronicles 10-29	David the King
2 Chronicles 1-9	Solomon the King
2 Chronicles 10-36	The Monarchy (especially Judah) through the destruction and the exile

INDICES

SUBJECT INDEX

BIBLICAL INDEX

[Page numbers in bold numeral indicate extended discussions of the text; specific citations within these sections are not indicated].

GPH